HOW TO GROW A SCHOOL GARDEN

HOW TO GROW A
School Garden

Arden Bucklin-Sporer and
Rachel Kathleen Pringle

TIMBER PRESS
Portland * London

Frontispiece: A community of gardeners. *Photo by Brooke Hieserich*
Photographs are by the authors unless otherwise indicated.

Lesson plans from *The Growing Classroom* by Roberta Jaffe and Gary Appel
(Addison-Wesley 2001). Developed by Life Lab Science and the National Garden-
ing Association. Reprinted with permission from the National Gardening Association,
South Burlington, Vermont.

Lesson plans from Earth Steward Gardener Curriculum reprinted with permission from
Cultivating Community, Portland, Maine.

Lesson plans reprinted with permission from Life Lab Science Program,
Santa Cruz California.

Lesson plans reprinted with permission from The Watershed Project, Richmond,
California.

Published in 2010 by Timber Press, Inc.

The Haseltine Building
133 S.W. Second Avenue, Suite 450
Portland, Oregon 97204-3527
www.timberpress.com

2 The Quadrant
135 Salusbury Road
London NW6 6RJ
www.timberpress.co.uk

ISBN-13: 978-1-60469-000-2

Printed in China
Third Printing 2012

Library of Congress Cataloging-in-Publication Data
Bucklin-Sporer, Arden.
  How to grow a school garden : a complete guide for parents and teachers / Arden
Bucklin-Sporer and Rachel Kathleen Pringle.
     p. cm.
  Includes bibliographical references and index.
  ISBN 978-1-60469-000-2
  1. School gardens. I. Pringle, Rachel Kathleen. II. Title.
  SB55.B83 2010
  635—dc22   2009051601

A catalog record for this book is also available from the British Library.

To Mom, who had
the good sense to send
us outside to play.
—*Arden*

To Mom and Dad,
who decided to raise
us on the farm.
—*Rachel*

CONTENTS

Preface 9

Introduction 13

1. WHY SCHOOL GARDENS? 23

2. LAYING THE GROUNDWORK 37

3. GETTING THE MOST FROM YOUR SITE:
    DESIGN CONSIDERATIONS 47

4. GROUNDBREAKING, BUDGETING, AND FUNDRAISING 71

5. DEVELOPING YOUR SCHOOL GARDEN PROGRAM 85

6. A HEALTHY OUTDOOR CLASSROOM 103

7. TRICKS OF THE TRADE 117

8. PLANTING, HARVESTING, AND COOKING
    IN THE GARDEN 131

9. YEAR-ROUND GARDEN LESSONS AND ACTIVITIES 149

10. A DECADE IN A SCHOOL GARDEN: ALICE FONG YU
    ALTERNATIVE SCHOOL, SAN FRANCISCO, CALIFORNIA ... 171

School Garden Recipes 185

Example of State Content Standards 195

Resources 197

Bibliography 215

Index 221

Eager students line up for garden time. *Photo by Brooke Hieserich*

PREFACE

Parents are the engines that drive any schoolyard transformation, so this book speaks most directly to them—to you. Teachers, too, are essential to the ongoing success of these projects, so we hope that this book will inspire and help educators bring an excitement about school gardens into their classrooms, and guide parents toward a meaningful involvement in school garden projects and their larger school community. School gardens are a collective effort; this book shows you how to maximize and sustain the energy within your community.

The first half of this book is about creating and developing the garden space, while the second half provides guidance for school garden programs. Building a school garden is a very accomplishable project. Developing strategies that sustain it over time, however, is infinitely more complex. In addition to guiding the transformation from schoolyard to school garden, this book describes the organizational structures that will keep it relevant, vibrant, and well utilized over time.

In the following chapters you will discover ways to get your community involved, how to raise funds and budget for a garden program, ideas on how to design a garden to best fit your site, what building materials there are to choose from, and a full section of recipes for cooking in the garden. We've also provided tried and true "tricks of the trade" (chapter 7) to help you get ahead of the game: must-have materials, creative solutions to common challenges (such as watering with a group of kindergartners), and strategies to manage and channel the energy of a class of eager and enthusiastic students.

Throughout the book, we've provided quick tip sheets or to-do lists for tasks and challenges common to any school garden, such as what to do with a recalcitrant principal, how to promote a school garden, or how to stock a tool shed. We've also provided examples of materials produced by actual school gardens, including a program overview and garden plan presented to a school community considering a potential garden project; a sample school garden budget; an annual fund letter sent to potential donors in the community; and a sample of a school garden newsletter. (Please note that names and identifying characteristics of actual individuals and institutions have been changed on all of these documents to protect their privacy.)

Parents and teachers dedicated to connecting gardening to the curriculum will find inspiration and practical guidance throughout this book. We've provided samples of how to link garden-based lessons to standards, and how to evaluate the scope and sequence of a particular grade level or subject area with classroom teachers to incorporate lessons in the outdoor classroom. In chapter 9, "Year-Round Garden Lessons and Activities" we've provided some of our favorite garden lessons and lists of seasonal activities; and extensive resources for garden curricula, support, and supplies are listed in the back of the book. While the school garden is a rich environment for learning in and of itself, it also serves as an introduction to a much broader understanding of the natural world. Connecting students to a school garden can be the beginning of environmental stewardship. We hope to plant the seed that helps your project flourish.

Many years of trial and error with school gardens in the San Francisco Unified School District are behind the writing of this book. We have worked closely with school sites and garden coordinators, with teachers and principals, and with the amazing kindergarten through eighth grade students in SFUSD. They continue to be our muse. We have also worked with facilities departments, landscape crews, volunteers, parent groups, and other school garden support organizations across the country. Throughout the book, we've shared some first-person accounts of our own experience in San Francisco school gardens. We hope these stories shed some light on what it is like to be a parent building a new garden program from the ground up, or a teacher trying to harness the wonder and excitement of children at work in their garden.

A school garden is part of an ecosystem that includes students and the school community. Like any ecosystem, it is a complex twining of different life forms: a class of first graders is just one of those life forms in a school garden. Teachers, parents, students, soil bacteria, plant material, endosperm, blackbirds, Jerusalem crickets, roly-polies, and weather systems are all actors on the school garden stage, affecting one another, jostling for positions. Of course each garden is different, springing from the grass roots efforts of a school community.

Our aim is to help establish the organizing principles for any school garden, no matter how different they may look. We also want to share the lessons we have learned about how to manage and sustain a school garden by growing the community around it. Good luck and happy gardening!

ACKNOWLEDGMENTS

Many have come before us, and hopefully many more will continue to refine and expand the use of the natural world in the classroom. There is no doubt that much of what we talk about in this book are ideas that we stumbled upon by reading other books about school gardening, or attending conferences about school gardening and environmental education, or visiting other cities and states that are working toward similar goals. It is difficult to trace those first seeds that grew into an inspiration.

We acknowledge, sadly, that we aren't acknowledging everyone, but we are thankful for the great ideas from Suzy Peacock and Real School Gardens in Fort Worth, Texas; our friends at the Boston Schoolyard Initiative; the wonderful folks from Evergreen in Canada who have shown us the way; and the Center for Ecoliteracy for the conference they held at the Edible Schoolyard in Berkeley, California, in 1997 that shined a spotlight on school gardens.

Thanks to Sharon Danks for her incredible vision and knowledge of this field, the Occidental Arts and Ecology Center and all the work they are doing to promote and sustain school gardens, Delaine Eastin for her immense contribution to school gardens in California, and the invaluable California School Garden Network.

Thank you to Nan McGuire and the wonderful board of the San Francisco Green Schoolyard Alliance for providing us with a platform upon which to enact this ongoing experiment. We are grateful to Annette Huddle for her collaboration, teaching, and knowledge; and to SFUSD broad-minded facilities people, namely David Goldin, Leonard Tom, Lori Shelton, Nik Kaestner, and all the Buildings & Grounds folks who are critical to the ongoing successes of San Francisco school gardens.

Thanks to Liana Szeto who gave us our heads but held on to the reins.

We are grateful to Juree Sondker who approached us with this idea, to our copyeditor, Carolyn Holland, and to all the team at Timber Press.

Many thanks to all the garden coordinators in San Francisco who are doing the great work of educating our students to be excellent stewards of our future, with special thanks to Ayesha Ercelawn, Christine Leishman, Jean Moshofsky-Butler, Linda Myers, Amy Mack, and Diana Samuelson.

We are thankful for our families (Karl, Sam, Jack, and August for Arden; and Jim, Jane, Abigail, and Dwight for Rachel) who have put up with and supported us during the months of writing this book.

Grateful acknowledgments to Life Lab, Cultivating Community, and the National Gardening Association for sharing their excellent curriculum; to Laurel Anderson of Salmon Creek School in Occidental for her recipes and model garden program; to Nora Brereton for her curriculum connections; and to Stephanie Ma, Ayesha Ercelawn, and Brooke Hieserich for so many fantastic photographs.

Students water with the help of the garden coordinator.

INTRODUCTION

A school garden is an outdoor classroom oasis, attracting countless organisms, each a rich opportunity to teach students about the complex and fascinating ecosystem that we are all a part of. School gardens provide on-site "field trip" opportunities for students, even in the most resource-deficient schools. School gardens may be as small as raised boxes on the asphalt play yard or planter boxes on a rooftop garden. In some cases, a school may have the space to take over an unused playing field or parking lot and turn it into a mini-farm with chickens and even goats or sheep. School gardens may be designed to help students learn about food and nutrition by planting edible crops, or lessons might focus on the local habitat by planting native plants. The common denominator of all school gardens, however, is that various

Students inspect the calendulas.

A harvest party. *Photo by Stephanie Ma*

classes utilize them as outdoor classrooms. The class may be planned as a standards-based lesson that charts the growth of recently planted fava bean plants and measures the change in growth over time. Or more typically, the focus of the class might veer unexpectedly toward pollination, due to the unanticipated arrival of a hummingbird nectaring in the pineapple sage. In both cases, school garden lessons are connected to education standards.

It is no wonder that school gardens have been in existence for over a century and are presently regaining popular appeal. Historically, victory gardens and school gardens supported families in times of war by providing more calories. Since that early part of the twentieth century, our nutritional needs have clearly shifted—presently society has a surfeit of calories, but a tremendous need for better nutrition.

The present generation of school age children is largely disconnected from agriculture, nutrition, and in many cases, alarmingly distant from the natural world. As parents, guardians, and citizens of this world, we look for ways to fix this complex problem. We know we cannot expect children to care about local, not to mention distant, environmental problems when they have no connection to their own. A school garden can begin the process of finding a solution to these complex problems. Connecting children to the natural world by growing food or building native habitat gardens may give them the capacity to care about their local ecology and perhaps even larger environmental issues.

A school garden grows in an urban elementary play yard. It is wedged between the climbing structure, the flagpole, and the basketball hoops— another feature interrupting the wide horizontal expanse of schoolyard blacktop. The garden has recently been built, but already it has the great aesthetic appeal of rowdy and untamed plants vying for space. The range and variety of plantings suggests a laboratory, as does the blackboard and measuring equipment left out after yesterday's class. Although not large, the garden has great depth, as student investigations into the mysteries and miracles of soil, microorganisms, and root patterns will attest. Looking skyward, there are opportunities to study clouds, weather patterns, and the insects and birds that are drawn to the garden's leafy green shade. In this small patch of recently exposed earth, vegetables grow—lettuce, carrots, and broccoli planted by students who wait eagerly to taste their efforts.

It has been a remarkable experience to witness how few urban children have a connection to their own ecosystems. More remarkable, however, is how quickly they are able to establish deep bonds with nature when they are given the opportunity. The old adage "getting your hands in the dirt" is literally what students do in a school garden, and often it is the first time they have done so. Once they are engaged in this simple act, worlds are suddenly opened up. Distinguishing between "dirt" and "dirty" takes some explaining but once permission is given to engage hands, or tools, with dirt, all sorts of notions about what peers may think evaporate. It can, of course, be washed off.

There is a large gap between what public schools have and what they need. Parents have a great opportunity to help fill this gap. There are many ways to do this, but it usually boils down to either giving time or money to your children's school. School gardens require a little of each and are an excellent and inexpensive way to add value to a school site. Gardens are also a platform on which to build community. Enriching a school on so many different levels, a garden program is a gentle rebellion of sorts—an antidote to the sour note of diminishing resources. Many parents are unsure of how to be involved in their child's school and the school garden is an excellent interface, especially for parents who have recently arrived in this country and are excited to share their knowledge and particular ways of agriculture.

In many ways a school garden program fills the huge void left by the disappearance of home economics curricula from our schools. The valuable life skills from that curriculum, such as resourcefulness and

School gardens are vibrant and kid-centered.

thrift, or how to cook and shop with good nutrition in mind, or how to sit and share a meal with other people, basic civility, and even table manners, can be illustrated to some degree in a school garden. Cooking and eating from the garden might have been part of the daily life half a century ago, but it is a truly remarkable and novel experience for urban students now. A typical afternoon garden class might easily include a harvest party: students are called upon to select, harvest, wash, and cook a particular crop for their classmates. The class serves one another and sits down to eat together. While some might be surprised to see a group of second graders enjoying a snack of chopped chard sautéed in garlic and olive oil, the simple fact is that children will eat what they grow. Parents are *always* surprised to see their young children eating vegetables at school that they have had no luck serving at home. Some students become veritable vegetable snobs and will only eat freshly harvested baby lettuces and organic garlic, much to the amusement of all of us.

School gardens are springing up everywhere from Albuquerque, New Mexico, to Sidney, Australia. Each school garden is as different as the next, arising from the particular vision and efforts of students, parents, teachers, and community members. As varied as school gardens are, the organizational constructs that sustain them tend to evolve in a parallel fashion. The gardens we have grown to know in Texas, Massachusetts, Ontario, and California, and Devon, England, have remarkably similar strategies for sustainability, each having arrived at their particular formula by themselves. The plants and ecosystems will differ from place to place, however the underpinnings of support for an institutional garden remain similar everywhere. This book is an attempt to articulate that formula.

We suggest that all notions of aesthetic fussiness and perfection be released, as they have no place in a school garden. Rows of carrots will be imperfect, wheelbarrows will tip, and dirt will fly. Plant enough to share with the inevitable critters that will take up residence (a little tolerance is a good thing) and know that when you aren't looking, the tiny carrots will be plucked one after another in search for that one big one. Ask the students to paint the signs and label the beds; the more kid-centered your school garden is, the more the students will feel like kings in their kingdom. The overall appearance of the school garden should have a rambunctious, robust kind of beauty. This book is based on the assumption that if you are starting a garden, there is a basic understanding of horticulture or gardening. If you are lacking these skills, there are many opportunities through local master gardener programs, cooperative extensions, community college, or university classes to learn them. And remember not to be intimidated by lack of knowledge. The most useful thing a student can hear an adult say is "I don't know the answer to your question, but let's go find out."

In this book, we approach the management of a school garden much in the same way one might manage a school library. As each class has library time and cycles in and out each week, they will cycle through their school garden. Both these institutions are often stewarded by a parent or a part-time staff person. School gardens are, in fact, libraries full of life, mystery, and surprise.

Sometimes there's just not enough to do on an asphalt schoolyard.

A HISTORY OF SCHOOL GARDENS

Since everything that enters into human understanding comes through the senses, the first reason of man is a reason of the senses. . . . Our first masters of knowledge are our feet, our hands, and our eyes.
—Jean Jacques Rousseau, *On Education*

The concept of a school garden is far from new. Numerous studies and papers on gardens as an educational tool chronicle its evolution from the eighteenth century in Europe to its modern-day existence on both sides of the Atlantic. Various prominent philosophers emphasized direct sensory experience as the cornerstone of education, from Rousseau (1712–1771) to Friedrich Froebel (1782–1852), the developer of the kindergarten education movement. In Austria in 1879 Erasmus Schwab published *The School Garden: Being a Practical Contribution to the Subject of Education* as a tool for enforcing a law that mandated gardens in schools (Desmond, Grieshop, and Subramaniam 2003). In the United States, the first school garden was created in 1891 at the George Putnam School in Roxbury, Massachusetts. And as the United States moved into the twentieth century, school gardens (as well as community gardens and victory gardens) were flourishing as

School gardens are often whimsical.

a result of war efforts and various Progressive era educational reforms (Trelstad 1997). Daniel Desmond, James Grieshop, and Aarti Subramaniam of the University of California at Davis have summarized the massive amount of research about the global history and present outcomes of the school garden movement in their paper prepared for the Food and Agriculture Organization of the United Nations, "Revisiting Garden-Based Learning in Basic Education" (2004). They cite three peaks in U.S. national interest in school gardens: 1900–1930, a time of Progressive reforms and war mobilization; 1960–1970, coun-

Spring in the school garden. *Photo by Stephanie Ma*

ter-cultural and environmental movements; and 1990–2000, a period of renewed interest in education reform and environmental education. We might add that another peak in interest is happening right now with the current attention on climate change, efforts to reconnect children to the natural world, and heightened awareness of sustainability issues and green practices.

It is important to recognize that there is a deep history to the school garden concept. By beginning your own project, you are continuing to promote a method of teaching that incorporates many long-held values such as hard work, discipline, cooperation, and self-awareness. You are also promoting an education that fosters an awareness of nature, agriculture and nutrition, and community. Other school communities around the globe are doing similar projects to enrich and improve their children's educational settings and nutrition. The motivations behind the past century of efforts remain the same.

A CALL TO ARMS: BEING A PARENT IN THE PUBLIC SCHOOL COMMUNITY

If your public school district is anything like ours, your district administrators and public school principals are called on to do more with less. They are asked to get by with fewer teachers, make do without the school librarian, cut custodial hours, provide a less expensive lunch for students, or cut landscaping crew hours. Most administrators will do everything in their power to keep budget cuts out of the classroom, and typically the school facility and the enrichment programs take the brunt.

Most schoolyards in urban districts are entirely capped in asphalt because it is maintenance free, and fewer staff are needed to supervise the wide horizontal spaces at recess time. On asphalt yards, recess play becomes the domain of play structures, whizzing balls, and competitive games. While this fierce activity is beneficial for students who need to let off steam, providing a variety of play options on both hard and softscape reduces competition for game space and balls. And as parents, we long for something natural for our children to engage with during their school day. We envision trees and shade, borders of living plants, raised beds spilling over with crops, logs or boulders, and the robust beauty of a more natural schoolyard ecosystem.

By digging in and being part of your child's education through the development of a school garden ecosystem, you are engaging in a grass-roots rebellion against the status quo of asphalt and bare-bones learning. It is a positive and deeply hopeful investment in your community, school, and children. Establishing a garden at your children's school is like a modern barn raising, calling on the participation and talents of a diverse group of parents, teachers, and others in the community to create an oasis that quickly will become the heart of the school. It will provide countless opportunities to teach students about the environment and the natural world in which we live. For very little investment, great value can be added to both the school site and to the environmental consciousness of a new generation of students.

The organizational talents, community-building abilities, and financial support of parents provide the padding on the bones of your neighborhood school. Ask any principal of a well-functioning public school how she gets through the day, and she will likely tell you her school runs smoothly thanks to her professional staff and the families of the children in the school who support her. These families generously give their time and money to vital programs that enrich their children's school day.

Being actively involved in your child's public school is rewarding and a wonderful way to bond to your community. It is an excellent education in democracy, and a great window into the world of public administration, local government, and neighborhood politics. And, as a parent, developing a school garden program is a fantastic way to engage with your public school and introduce a new generation of children to the magic and the ecology of a school garden.

This book will provide a step-by-step explanation on how to be an effective public school parent and positively engage with your local school administration while developing a much cherished and valuable learning tool, the school garden.

1.

WHY SCHOOL GARDENS?

There is rising concern over a growing divide between children and the ecology that surrounds them. More and more commonly children stay inside sitting in front of computers or video games, exploring virtual reality instead of playing and exploring out of doors. The reasons for this are well documented and widely discussed. Parents have become more protective due to a perceived fear of danger in the outdoors (Clements 2004, 68–80); the introduction of the automobile and a dramatic increase in its usage over the last century has resulted in a lack of play spaces in the streets (Karsten 2005, 275–290); major demographic shifts have occurred in the last century resulting in a dramatic reduction of the number of families who live on farms; and kids are now bombarded with irresistible forms of media and electronic entertainment resulting in more time spent indoors (Roberts, Foehr, and Rideout 2005; Rideout and Hamel 2006). In urban areas, the relative scarcity of empty lots, parks, and natural open space makes connection with the natural world even more tenuous for many kids. The consequences of this disconnect have been considered by academics, journalists, educational professionals, politicians, and environmentalists. Are children gaining a sense of the systems at large if they aren't outside exploring them? Are children learning to be independent problem solvers if they aren't afforded the opportunity to engage their hearts, minds, and hands by building a fort somewhere outside using raw materials and their own creativity? Are they suffering from Attention Deficit Disorder and increased incidence of obesity due to a lack of unstructured play and activity outside? In response, education professors have written on the positive, lifelong effects of nature

Taking the curriculum to the outdoor classroom.

Students fill the new beds with soil.

play; journalist Richard Louv wrote *Last Child in the Woods, Saving our Children from Nature Deficit Disorder* and cofounded the Children and Nature Network; "No Child Left Inside" legislation is being brought before Congress; and a tapestry of environmental organizations strive to draw children and families away from the TV and into the outdoors. And what about our *schools*? Are we able to move beyond the plastic play structure and re-imagine the schoolyard to incorporate nature play and a small slice of the natural world? Can we build a hands-on outdoor classroom that amplifies the math, science, and language arts that are taught inside?

School gardens provide a space for students to reconnect to the ecology around them. Gardens teach students about agriculture, how we nourish ourselves, the importance of stewardship, and an appreciation for the natural systems that support life on our planet. In this chapter we will discuss the importance of school gardens as an experiential, hands-on educational tool where core curriculum comes alive. We will explore the accepted research about the benefits of school garden programs, which extol the virtues of experimental, kid-centered, not-so-orderly gardening that fosters keen observation, critical and independent thought, and the achievement of life skills. We will also share a few thoughts on the value of unstructured and imaginative nature play in the schoolyard.

Each spring my fourth and fifth grade classes would come to the garden and inevitably beg to do "The Mississippi River," an activity that had become a tradition in the garden. Over time I persuaded them to call it "The Colorado River" as what was formed by our experiment was much more erosive, canyonlike, and definitively western than its midwestern counterpart. At the top of the hill I would turn on the water letting it course down the sandy slope, along the beds and into the digging area. A riverbed was rudimentarily formed with a little help from the students, trowels in hand. Some of the students built towns and cities along the banks with stones and sticks, some created a large reservoir at the end, and others diverted some of the river farther away to water crops (represented by pine needles and leaves) or nurture growing towns. And the river kept running. At some point during the activity, however, the water would slow to a trickle and the students would eventually stop their bustling. Hey! What happened to the water?! We would investigate; sometimes the culprits were the increasing number of diversions to the new settlements that were happening upstream, sometimes the "snow pack" up at the top of the hill was too low to create a strong enough river to supply all those downstream. The water would occasionally get very strong, too, wiping out towns in the "flood zone" and creating braids in the river and deep canyons.

Eventually I would turn off the water and our discussion would ensue: water is a creator of landforms, water is a resource, water is finite, and water can be a destroyer of property. What are the problems in this tiny world we've created? What are the solutions? How are landforms created? What is beautiful about them? This simple activity that was the epitome of fun for the students also came embedded with countless lessons that chipped away at academic requirements. And the garden was the ideal place for such a messy endeavor. Finally, the reservoir was emptied and the water brought to our native garden. We carried small buckets of sand from downhill to fill in the river bed and canyons, repairing the fissured ground. —RKP

GARDEN-BASED LEARNING AND EXPERIENTIAL EDUCATION

Learning in the garden happens through direct experience and experimentation. Crops are allowed to reseed themselves; pumpkins left to the elements provide an opportunity for students to observe rot, decay, and eventual redemption as the next generation of seed germinates. Children investigate the creation of landforms by allowing water to run down a sandy slope. School gardens are outdoor classrooms that introduce a trial-and-error approach to learning; hands engage the mind to problem solve with tangible results. Garden-based learning

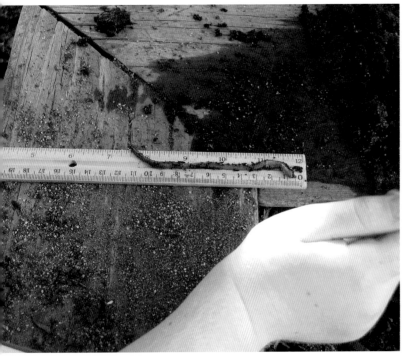

A living math problem. *Photo by Ayesha Ercelawn*

Soil exploration in the outdoor classroom. *Photo by Stephanie Ma*

can be minimally defined as "an instructional strategy that utilizes a garden as a teaching tool."(Desmond, Grieshop, and Subramaniam 2003). This definition doesn't fully illustrate an outdoor classroom's multiple approaches to achieving student comprehension, however. Traditional classrooms are often tightly structured and regulated by a school's mandate to teach to the education standards. School gardens as outdoor classrooms *also* teach to the curriculum, but, by nature, are dynamic educational settings that provide numerous opportunities to expand upon the standards. Caring for a seedling from germination to maturity, observing hummingbirds pollinate salvia, smelling a sprig of thyme, weeding, and many other *direct* experiences are integral to a young child's developing sense of the world around him. By learning through action and through stimulation of *all* the senses, the school garden amplifies and enhances subjects covered in the traditional classroom. Gardens also teach students that learning may take place everywhere, and especially so *out* of the classroom.

THE BENEFITS OF SCHOOL GARDENS—MAKING THE CASE

The benefits of school gardens are many and the evidence has been corroborated by a diverse group of practitioners and researchers. Numerous studies point to school gardens as a means of improving academic achievement, promoting healthy lifestyles, demonstrating the principles of stewardship, encouraging community and social development, and instilling a sense of place. In this section we will mention some of the studies that have substantiated these benefits on the academic, nutritional, environmental, community and individual levels. Evidence such as this will help you make the case for your school garden project and is useful when confronted by a reluctant principal or school district. A review of the current relevant research will help you build the foundation of your project.

The first kindergarten class that came to the garden in the fall after I began teaching was a quick and dirty introduction to working with five year olds in the outdoors. I remember hearing their chatter as they ascended through the campus to where I was waiting in the garden. Once inside the gate their somewhat orderly line disintegrated into a loose train of bouncing bodies and pointing hands. They batted the apples on the branches and shrieked as they quickly drew their hands back from the buzzing bees on the ceanothus; one little girl ran directly to a tall bunch of cosmos waving in the sun and plucked two flower tops off with each hand, turned around and beamed at me as she sat down with her classmates on the straw bales. I stood a bit bewildered; thank goodness kindergarten class only lasted thirty minutes instead of the usual forty-five.

In time I learned the art of kindergarten instruction by observing veteran teachers calmly focus their erratic masses. I discovered the pure joy of seeing these first-time gardeners completely rapt by the simplest of natural wonders; pulling a carrot out of the ground for the very first time produced eyes so big and a look so astonished I couldn't help but be swept up in the miracle myself. In these moments with the youngest of our students I developed my belief in the power of the garden as an outdoor classroom; they absorbed everything they experienced. In the next garden class the students calmly watched the bees, they called the ceanothus by name, and after exploring the parts of plants that we eat, carrots became known as those "yummy orange roots."—RKP

School gardens enhance academic achievement

Several studies suggest that school gardens and outdoor classrooms enhance student achievement, especially in elementary education. As a form of environmental education, gardening has been shown to improve performance in math, science, writing, social studies, and overall attitudes toward learning. School gardens are living laboratories, libraries, problem sets and equations. They provide the muse for writing a poem. They supply the data for the graph that creates the

School gardens inspire cooperation.

equation on how fast the plants are growing. Through their dynamic nature, gardens embody a genuine and direct experimental, inquiry-based approach to learning. Compelling results have emerged from the research.

Texas A&M University conducted several studies on science achievement in relation to garden-based learning. As noted in the abstract of Growing Minds (2005), science achievement of third, fourth, and fifth grade elementary students (ages seven to eleven) was studied using a sample of 647 students from seven elementary schools in Temple, Texas. As part of their science curriculum, students in the experimental group participated in school gardening activities in addition to using traditional indoor, classroom-based lessons. In contrast, students in the control group were taught science using the traditional methods only. The study found that students in the experimental group scored significantly higher on the science achievement test compared to the students in the control group (Klemmer, Waliczek, and Zajicek 2005, 448–52).

The 1998 study sponsored by numerous state departments of education "Closing the Achievement Gap: Using the Environment as an Integrated Context for Learning," found that youth who experienced curricula in schools where the environment served as the primary classroom, school gardens included, faired better on standardized measures of achievement in math, reading, language, and spelling (Lieberman and Hoody 1998).Two similar studies followed in 2000 and 2005, in which the positive findings were consistent with the original study (State Education and Environment Roundtable [SEER] 2000; 2005).

The National Gardening Association conducted a study of third and fifth grade classrooms using GrowLab, a curriculum that incorporates either a greenhouse or an in-classroom germination station where students observe a plant's growth from seed. GrowLab classrooms scored higher in student understanding of life science concepts and science inquiry skills than classrooms that did not use GrowLab lessons (Pranis 1992). School gardens are outdoor laboratories where plant growth from seed can be observed directly and experimented with; students learn first-hand how to formulate, on a daily basis, a hypothesis and test it. Will the seed grow if I don't give it water? What if I shade it from any light by accidentally mulching it in? Will the seed germinate if I plant it in early December?

It is worth noting that school gardens provide the necessary landscape for multiple learning styles among groups of students. Teachers who venture into this new setting might discover a different strength revealed in a student who was previously struggling. School gardens provide a space to easily and safely break from the traditional teaching and learning patterns of the indoor classroom.

Every year there were a few students who would make the teachers sigh and shake their heads at the mention of their names. Inside, these students could not sit still, were perpetually distracted, and hard to manage. Even in the garden, maintaining their attention remained difficult. Occasionally, though, one of these energetic students would find a niche in the garden classroom. They would thrive; needing only one explanation of how to thin the rows of carrots, they would meticulously finish an entire bed without supervision. The garden was their medium, their space where excess energy was funneled into solving a problem with their hands. —RKP

School gardens promote healthy lifestyles

Countless studies show a dramatic increase in childhood obesity and there is significant and warranted alarm over what this indicates for our future (Troiano et al. 1995; Ogden et al. 2006). Children benefit enormously from a working knowledge of good nutrition and healthy lifestyle choices, and this is compellingly taught in a school garden.

The bulk of the studies conducted on the benefits of school gardens relate to their overwhelmingly positive influence on students' nutritional awareness and practices. Experiences in the garden infinitely improve student's knowledge about and attitudes toward eating vegetables, and also increase their consumption of these foods. From learning to cook fresh vegetables and enjoying a meal with friends, to the hard, physical work of maintaining a garden, students begin to learn pleasurable and positive life-sustaining habits.

A study published in 2007 found that sixth grade student involvement in a garden-based nutrition education program resulted in an increase in their fruit and vegetable consumption by 2½ servings per day, more than twice their overall fruit and vegetable consumption. Hands-on gardening and the sheer proximity to fruits and vegetables in the program significantly influenced food-choice behavior among the students (McAleese and Rankin 2007, 662–665). Another study found that fourth grade students who received garden-based nutrition education were more willing to try certain vegetables than students who received nutrition education without the hands-on garden component; and that their positive attitudes continued for at least six months after the lessons were taught (Morris and Zidenberg-Cherr 2002, 91–93).

Parent after parent would stop me in the hallway, or at school events to tell me that their previously vegetable-hating child was now eating salad at home. Despite the complaints, they said, of not having the "sauce"—the students' term for the vinaigrette we made in the garden—at home, salad was being consumed where it hadn't been before. I always found that students who planted, cared for, harvested, and prepared their own food loved it, no matter if it was a bowl of lettuce, sautéed chard, or a handful of carrots. Harvest day was just too exciting to not get swept up in the magic of the process; eating was the ultimate coup.—RKP

Several studies show that students who grow their own food are much more likely to eat fresh fruits and vegetables or express a preference for these foods (Libman 2007 87–95; Lineberger and Zajicek 2000, 593–597). Any garden coordinator who harvests, cooks, and eats with students in a school garden will corroborate this evidence in a heartbeat.

Beyond exposing students to fresh vegetables, school gardening also requires physical work. Simply spending time in the garden pulling weeds, searching for clues in a scavenger hunt, or mulching the beds with compost or straw necessitates activity and movement. Vastly

Students weeding sidewalk basins around a school. *Photo by Stephanie Ma*

- -

Students eating freshly harvested carrots.

different from sitting in a chair behind a desk, outdoor classrooms are inherently kinetic and instill a bodily awareness that is so important to discover in oneself at a young age. Creating a positive and easy-going atmosphere around physical activity can have effects that last a lifetime.

School gardens instill an environmental stewardship ethic

Every school, whether rural, suburban, or urban, resides within a watershed and within an ecosystem. Be it a neighborhood of concrete sidewalks or a vast woodland that surrounds a school, water, waste, and energy flow into and out of the system at large. These systems can be clearly demonstrated in a school garden. Numerous student-led activities play a role in a school's ecological footprint: composting food scraps and green waste in the worm bin, mulching garden beds with last year's straw bale seating, watering the plants with rainwater harvested from the roof of the shed, and picking up trash that has been strewn around the school (and then depositing it in the bin marked "landfill"). Understanding and caring for the ecosystem in which a school resides instills a strong environmental stewardship ethic. The mindfulness taught at school is then transported home to another neighborhood and another watershed, and so on.

Research derived from an intergenerational gardening project (pairing students and elders in the garden) in 2007 showed an increased consciousness of ecology and stewardship in the students who participated. The students expressed an interest in caring for the environment and an understanding of the interconnectedness within nature as an ecological principle (Mayer-Smith and Peterat 2007, 77–85). Another study conducted in Texas showed that second and fourth grade students who were part of a school garden program had significantly stronger positive environmental attitudes than students who were not (Skelly and Zajicek 1998, 579–583).

School gardens encourage community and social development

Life skills such as teamwork, volunteerism, self-understanding, leadership, decision-making ability, and communication skills are often cited as products of garden-based learning. A survey of third through fifth graders who participated in a gardening program for one year showed significant increases in self-understanding and in their ability to work in groups (Robinson and Zajicek 2005, 453–457). These talents are vital to the development of the health of an individual, not to mention a strong community. Students and teachers sit under a tree with the salad they've served each other, eating together and engaging in conversation. Older students complete community service hours in the garden, mentoring younger students or helping to sweep and organize the shed. And the garden becomes a centerpiece of many relationships within the school as the community organizes parties, workdays, and fundraisers to support it.

School gardens instill a sense of place

Our sense of place, or surrounding habitat, has become less clearly defined as uncontrolled development devours landscapes throughout the world. A sense of place is fundamental to our understanding of who we are. What the natural world looks, feels, and smells like on our part of the planet, helps us distinguish how we are the same and how we are different from the rest of the world. How will kids grow to care about larger planetary issues such as climate change or diminishing rainforests if they can't appreciate their own place on this earth? Developing a sense of place is critical to a foundation of ecological awareness and responsibility.

Many factors inform what grows in a habitat: weather, soil, geology, topography, cultural traditions, and history. All of these concepts are readily described in a school garden. There are many lessons that may highlight concepts that are place-based, such as studying the native peoples of your particular area, discerning what type of soil or substrate your garden is on, or observing what part of the city your garden is in and what creatures visit it. With lessons such as these, school gardens are models of place-based education, outdoor classrooms that will foster the next generation of environmental stewards.

It was interesting to note how the lessons in the garden expanded outwardly into the world. Students quickly recognized that the invasive plants that they spent time pulling in the school garden also existed in their own gardens. When we went to the nearby open spaces and parks, they were able to identify the same weeds and understand how they grew and interacted with the other native plants. —ABS

For students, going to the garden is an adventure. Ask them what they like most about the garden and they would say hunting for slugs and snails, creating imaginary worlds while digging in the spare bed, harvesting and eating salad, and simply being outside and allowed to explore during the school day. What is encouraging for educators about students' eagerness in this setting is that "garden time" *is* instructional time. The same concepts and standards that are covered in the traditional classroom come alive in the garden: students are counting and graphing the number of slugs versus snails, measuring the length of

Hunting for snails is a popular activity.

the spare bed, and discovering the vitamins and minerals in the leafy greens they are harvesting. Real experience with nature can lead to observations and reflections that are worked into more abstract concepts. Students help weed a bed and learn that these plants compete with crops for water and nutrients, and then later they understand the concept of spacing and thinning when tending a bed of beets. Tasting the nectar of the salvia flower requires an exploration of the relationship between plants and pollinators. Children learn first-hand about the systems at work around them, first directly and then more indirectly.

IMAGINATIVE AND UNSTRUCTURED NATURE PLAY

Beyond measures of academic achievement and research into the efficacy of gardens as a teaching tool, school gardens are spaces to stand slack-jawed in wonder at the natural world. School gardens are often whimsical and free-flowing in their design and layout. Upon entering, you might see odd hand-lettered signage indicating where the pond is, what bed is growing sunchokes and potatoes, and a temporary village built for garden fairies and gnomes. More and more people are discovering the importance of fostering a child's sense of wonder and imagination, and a school garden provides a platform for natural open-ended play.

A class of kindergarteners exploring the soil.

It was the end of the school year and the second grade was watering their bed of sunflowers, which had been germinated in peat cups in the windowsill of their classroom. Mari and Catherine noticed that several of the two-inch seedlings had been trampled and the stems were broken. They spent their free time carefully splinting the tiny sunflower plants with tiny sticks found in the mulch and yarn rummaged from the tool shed. They were deep into doctor play and I couldn't help but be impressed with the care and attention they gave to their patients. We were all particularly impressed the following September to see that the trampled sunflower plants had not only survived, but grown into seven-foot monsters—the only memory of the break was the bit of yarn still attached to the stems.—ABS

Schoolyard play options are commonly ball games such as basketball or dodgeball, or organized games, such as jump rope. The addition of a garden and nature play introduces a different more imaginative kind of play option that appeals to many students. Many studies reveal the values of unstructured play. All of them point to the cognitive benefits from play in nature, including creativity, problem-solving, focus, and self-discipline. The social and emotional benefits often include cooperation, flexibility, stress reduction, and reduced aggression (Burdette and Whitaker 2005; Kellert 2005).

Even the most sports-driven student can be observed abandoning his daily ritual of basketball to explore the fascinating pile of brush that had been pruned out of the oak tree. For days the first and second graders had been using that small pile of brush for inventive games. Pruned branches became peacock tails, forts, trains, brooms, and countless other inventions. Suddenly the basketball courts weren't so crowded, and the four square lines weren't so long.—ABS

RESEARCH AND EXISTING ORGANIZATIONS

More references and studies about the efficacy of school gardens for improving academic achievement, promoting healthy lifestyles, demonstrating the principles of stewardship, encouraging community and social development, and instilling a sense of place may be found in Resources in the back of this book. The California School Garden Network (www.csgn.org) has an extensive listing of research relating to garden-based learning and its influence on student achievement and ecoliteracy. The Children & Nature Network (www.childrenand-nature.org) also has an exhaustive list of research articles that substantiate much of the concern over children's lack of connection to the natural world, as well as the importance of fostering opportunities for reconnection. In the event that your community needs to justify the construction of a school garden, these references may be useful. By understanding the fundamental concepts and uses for including a school garden at your site, you are ready to begin the process of organizing and rallying support around the project.

A school garden program consists of many layers.

2.

LAYING THE GROUNDWORK

Before touching spade to earth there are many things to do to ensure the support, use, and sustainability of a school garden project. In this chapter we outline the first exploratory steps to help you get started in the process, and to help you understand if your school community is ready and ripe to begin the process. To cultivate long-term interest in the project, you'll need to develop a committee instead of taking it all on yourself. This chapter will provide ideas and examples of best practices to help streamline that process.

A schoolyard transformed.

DO YOUR HOMEWORK

As a first step, search the Internet for local and distant organizations that support garden-based learning. Spend time researching school gardens in your area, state, and country, starting with our listing of school garden organizations in the back of this book. In your search, use key words like "outdoor classroom" and "school garden." This all-important first step will help you understand what is already happening in the school garden arena, and will assist you in pitching it more effectively. It will also help you visualize and articulate your ideas. If other schools in your area already have gardens, make an appointment to see them, and take a good look at how their garden was developed and how it is used. In one meeting you will get a good list of dos and don'ts to set you out on the right foot. Often times you will find a knowledgeable person in the garden—either a teacher or parent—just by poking your head over the garden fence. Find out how they gathered administrative support for their garden project, and how a garden program is integrated into the school day. Most well-developed school gardens are delighted to share their experience, curriculum, and strategies with you, and seasoned school gardens will happily mentor a new and developing garden program. If you are the first in your area to build a garden, conduct a broader search in other counties, states, and even countries to formulate clear goals and objectives for your garden. By hooking into existing networks you will avoid reinventing the wheel, and save yourself a lot of time.

When I first decided to explore the possibility of building a school garden, I had no idea that my thinking was on a parallel track with so many other people. I had never heard of school gardens, and thought I had come up with this excellent idea by myself. What tremendous energy it took to create schedules, figure out what to teach, understand how to make it relevant to kids and their school day. As soon as I was able to reach out and realize that there was a larger movement of organizations interested in supporting children's access to the outdoors, nutrition, environmental education, and established school gardens, everything became simpler. We began to support one another, help out with new projects, communicate, socialize, and build a local movement together. —ABS

MAKE THE PITCH

The first task in building the foundation of a strong garden project is a sales pitch to the principal. Explaining the many levels in which a school garden program will support the school's curriculum will enlist the principal's interest and support—a critical component of any successful school garden project. Without it, it will be difficult to move the garden project forward. However, the power of the parent community is not to be underestimated—when used carefully and well it can garner the support of even the most hesitant administrators.

If you have already engaged and interested several teachers in the project, the principal will be more favorably inclined to endorse and influence the project. Enlisting the support of several teachers will help you make your case.

A principal will appreciate a thorough outline of how this garden will work in concert with other school programs, integrate with the core curriculum, and be of great use to the teachers as an outdoor classroom. Emphasize that the garden will be an asset to the school rather than a drain on classroom time and resources. Remember that one of the principal's core jobs is to support the teachers, and a school garden *will* support teachers by providing them with an additional classroom where curriculum literally comes alive. Included in this outline should be a preliminary design idea, a proposed garden location, a

EXAMPLE OF A SCHOOL GARDEN OVERVIEW

Benjamin Franklin Elementary School Garden

In an effort to explore the possibility of creating an outdoor learning garden for BFES, we have enlisted the support of staff and community members and researched standards-based curriculum that could be applied in the outdoor classroom.

Garden committee members
Joanne Puloski (1st grade parent)
Albert Cinceros (1st grade parent)
Mary Jane Jenson (3rd grade parent)
Reggie Jones (4th grade parent; member of PTA)

Teachers who have expressed interest in a garden program
Robert McNamee (3rd grade)
Sarah Collin, Roberta Myles, Jessica Fong (K)
Amanda Friend (2nd grade)

Possible curriculum to be used in the learning garden
The Growing Classroom, Life Lab
FOSS Science Kits K–5th

Location of garden site
The committee is investigating the possibility of putting a garden at the southwestern part of yard #1, or alternatively using the space to the west of the Special Education bungalow as an outdoor classroom. The next step would be to ascertain sunlight and water availability.

Maintenance of the site
Parents and students will construct the garden on a series of weekend workdays. Students will maintain raised beds, parents will organize several weekend workdays to improve and maintain the infrastructure.

Funding for the garden
The committee will request a small starter grant from the parent association, and then will write several grants for small amounts of funding. We will canvass the neighborhood and work with local businesses to build interest and support for our program. Our local hardware store has agreed to give the Benjamin Franklin School Garden 10 percent of their earnings on the first Monday of the month for a year. We expect to find more businesses that will contribute in a similar fashion.

construction timeline, and a stewardship and maintenance plan. Don't forget to include an annual budget and fundraising strategy. Describe both your funding plan and your long-term maintenance plan.

Our first grant to begin our school garden was thanks to our parent association. That original five hundred dollars gave us the opportunity to purchase some materials to set up the garden with raised beds and hoses, to make our outdoor classroom functional and inhabitable. Once established, we were able to begin to ask for funds from our newly established annual campaign to support us further. With something to show, we procured some small support from local businesses, and later began the process of developing a mission to seek funding from foundations. Our grass roots support and flexibility built a strong base upon which to grow. And our incremental approach to fundraising made the program sustainable from year to year. —ABS

We have found that most principals are easily brought on board and delighted to support a school garden when it is described as an outdoor classroom. However, because of often overwhelming work-loads, they may support the project, but don't want to be buried in an avalanche of details about it. Regular and concise reporting about the status of the project will go a long way in saving time and smoothing the way forward. It has been our experience that principals prefer to communicate in bullet points.

Principals touring a completed school garden project.

DEVELOP THE COMMITTEE

One of the best parts of starting a garden project is the wonderful opportunity it provides for collaboration with fellow parents. As your children's class and school is a magnificent jumble of ethnicities, personalities, abilities, and interests, so are the parents of those children. Finding a group to work together to provide different perspectives is the first step towards building a committee. Start by including everyone who would like to be part of the project, and it is likely that a committee leader and a handful of participants will emerge after a few meetings. Those who have neither the time nor passion will drop out. Reach out to people with widely differing talents, not just the

What to do with a recalcitrant principal:

» *Ask them to tour several successful local school gardens with you.*

» *Recruit teachers and parents as school garden advocates.*

» *Develop an organized and professional parent committee.*

» *Secure a small starter grant.*

» *Identify long-term sources of funding for the program.*

» *Find principals in other schools with successful garden programs and set up a dialogue.*

» *Develop a clear stewardship plan.*

obvious landscapers, horticulturalists, and gardeners; think about who might be a good writer, web developer, organizer, or neighborhood activist. Of course parents with strong backs and a willingness to take on physical work should be thrown into the mix. Collaboration and development of a broad base of parental support will sustain the garden project over time.

As we began to build our program, I made a point to be at pick up and drop off, in order to know which parents came to gather their children in trucks. Trucks are indispensable for helping with compost deliveries, straw bale delivery, and mulch drop off. I introduced myself to the truck owning parents and asked if they might be available to help out the garden program. I learned that parents are much more likely to agree to tasks when they are asked directly. I also kept a sharp eye out for telltale signs of gardening skills—a sighting of a set of Felco clippers in a leather holster on a dad picking up his kids was a dead giveaway.—ABS

Schedule formal meetings—at whatever interval works for the group. Setting them up in advance allows for better attendance. The development and careful cultivation of this parent committee will keep the garden project moving forward. Attention to developing a functioning, inclusive and *fun* garden committee will go a long way toward the continued success of your garden project.

E-mail groups such as YahooGroups are a great time-saving tool, and much committee work can be accomplished through these systems, but don't forget to schedule face time as well. A school garden committee—no different from any other group of people—is based on relationships, and taking the time to develop them is helpful.

Don't forget to ask the principal and several teachers to be part of the committee. We have seen projects derail when school staff is not included in the planning process. Staff can provide a much-needed sounding board and will insert a note of realism into the planning process. When parents meet without teacher input, the committee may be perceived as exclusive, which is counterproductive to school/garden/administration dynamics. Invite the principal to join. Quite often school staff is too busy to attend meetings, but they should be provided with a digest and asked for comments.

A parent committee discusses different garden design options.

Originally, as we were growing as a committee with just four members, we had potluck dinner meetings at our homes. It was a great opportunity to get to know one another more intimately, get out for that desperately needed night away from the parental grind, have a glass of wine, and begin to bond and trust one another. Sometimes we arranged field trips to other gardens in our area. As a result, that committee lasted for more than a decade, rotating new members in as families matriculated out of the school. More importantly, as our children head off to colleges, we remain close friends. —ABS

ARTICULATE THE GOALS OF THE SCHOOL GARDEN

As your garden committee develops, you will want to begin to articulate the goals of your garden. Each school garden might have a different set of goals; think about what you would like to accomplish (goals) and how you will get there (objectives). Careful consideration and articulation of what you would like your garden to accomplish and why will help you later in fundraising. A well-crafted set of goals will also help you communicate effectively to others about the benefits of a school garden.

Hands-on education.

TAKE THE LONG VIEW

It is human nature to want groundbreaking to begin immediately. Sometimes parents are driven by the fact that their students may be in the upper grades and they would like to see a garden during their tenure at the school. However, a planning process is an important step in the development of a school garden. At least six months or a year is advised as planning time. During this period, make sure that the teachers are consulted. If a teacher wants to teach water cycles, perhaps a pond with a roof water harvesting system would help illustrate these concepts. Other teachers might want beds with flowers for the study of pollination, and others might want to grow food crops. Spending some time clarifying how teachers would like to use their new outdoor classroom will go a long way toward ensuring its long-term sustainability.

EXAMPLE OF AN ANNUAL FUND LETTER

Dear Parents and Guardians of Benjamin Franklin Elementary School,

As school begins again each fall, we ask each family in our community to contribute to the Annual Fund. Your donation helps to insure the future of many unique enrichment programs for all students at Ben Franklin.

You and your children are the beneficiaries of academic excellence, a strong sense of community, and real life lessons. Annual funds enhance the educational experience of each child by providing:

* enrichment programs, such as performing artist workshops
* computers in each classroom along with technical support and supplies
* school sports programs
* professional development for the staff
* the development of a school-wide garden program
* school supplies, such as dictionaries, pens, pencils, and paper
* and so much more

Our goal is to have 100 percent participation, which means each family contributes what they are able. Please determine what level your family is comfortable with. As a guideline, we suggest a contribution of fifty dollars from families with one child at BFES, and one hundred dollars from families with two or more children in the school. If your family is able to give more, we welcome your generosity. However, no gift is too small!

Remember to check with your employer regarding matching fund opportunities. Many organizations will support your contribution by matching donations dollar for dollar. It's a great way to double your donation to our school!

We take pride in the accomplishments of the Ben Franklin teachers, administrators, parents, and students. It is our responsibility to ensure the future for our community. The Annual Fund is a critical piece of our support for the school.

A donation card is attached. If you have any questions or comments about the Annual Fund, matching fund donations, or about how our money is spent, please talk to a BFES parent board member. You may e-mail us at president@bfes.org, or call Joan Wister at (222) 234–1983.

With sincere thanks,

Joan Wister
Chair of Parent Association

Margaret Bootz
Principal, BFES

PRESENT YOUR PLAN TO THE PARENT ASSOCIATION OR SITE COUNCIL

Most schools have some kind of parent association, site council, or elected governing body who works in concert with the principal to shape school programming. It is important to outline your plans with these governing groups and cultivate their support. Request time at a meeting to present the expected outcomes of the garden project, its proposed budget, and a plan for sustaining it. We have found that a short slide show or Power Point presentation is a great tool. Annual fund drives are often conducted by the parent association. Public schools should all have an annual campaign drive, the goal being 100 percent participation. Participation can be as little as five dollars per family, but encouraging everyone—each and every family regardless of financial circumstances—to make a contribution to their child's education is a way to build meaningful community involvement. There is a kind of magic that occurs when parents give even a very small amount of money to support their student's education.

SECURE START-UP FUNDING

A small amount of money from the parent association can be the anchor for attracting more money from the outside community, and with parents doing most of the work; a little money can go a long way. Internal support for the program, evidenced by a small grant from the parent association will show the community that it is a coordinated, school-wide effort. The money can be used for construction expenses later on or for outreach, depending on the need. If you are finding that money from the school community is not forthcoming, it might be worth rethinking your outreach strategy. It might also mean that your school site is not ready for a garden, and it would be wise to wait for a more advantageous time.

Now that you have cultivated interest in the idea of a garden project, you are ready to begin to address basic design issues, site considerations, and develop strategies to build an interesting and dynamic garden project that will be sustained long into the future.

A well-designed school garden.

3.

GETTING THE MOST FROM YOUR SITE

Design Considerations

Taking time to plan and design a school garden is time well spent. Considering how the school garden will actually be used within the workings of the school is a critical step in the planning process. Often, people think of a garden as an aesthetic addition to the school's site, which it inevitably is, but more importantly it becomes an outdoor classroom, welcoming a variety of classes, enrichment programs, after-school activities, and community through its garden gate.

Design these outdoor classrooms for long-term success. One might be tempted to skip this phase and get right to the business of breaking ground, but attention to the points made in this chapter will ensure that the garden is sustained from year to year, long after the founding committee has moved on.

So far, you've fleshed out your idea and developed support for the garden project within the school community by:

» Connecting with other gardens in your area

» Cultivating principal buy-in

» Developing a committee to plan and move the project forward

» Understanding how the school staff would like to use the garden as an outdoor classroom

» Presenting a vision of your plan to the parent body

Now it is time to:

» Identify possible users of the outside space (teachers, parents, other groups)

» Involve the school district

» Conduct a site inventory

» Investigate start-up funding

» Consider the necessary elements for a school garden

» Get student input for the project

» Plan for groundbreaking

ENGAGE FUTURE USERS OF THE GARDEN IN THE DESIGN PROCESS

A school garden is essentially an institutional garden. Inviting interested teachers and students, as well as the varied school clubs and classes who may use it, to participate in the planning process will increase student interaction and build a stronger garden. Our colleagues from Real School Gardens in Fort Worth Texas have a simple equation: USE = SUSTAINABLILITY. Whatever a school site can do to increase the use of their garden, the more viable it will become.

We believe a garden with many layers of engagement will ultimately be sustained over time. If the fifth grade classes are studying pond ecology in the garden, the after-care kids are harvesting afternoon snacks and having salad parties, the neighbors are growing a kitchen

A spring garden party celebrates the entire community.

garden, and the parent association hosts their end-of-the-year party in the garden, you will know that you have built the layers of engagement that will sustain your school garden. The beauty of this system is that when one user group becomes inactive, the others will continue to support the project. When the school garden is the burden of one person or group, it becomes unstable and in danger of collapse. A supportive principal, who fully understands all the programs that take place in the school, will be able to brainstorm ideas with you on how to use the garden to its full capacity.

INVOLVE YOUR SCHOOL DISTRICT

Before you get too far in your planning, talk to your school district's Facilities Department and allow them to be included in the process of developing your garden plans. Whether your school district has a hundred sites or just one, it is useful to remember that the piece of ground you are going to alter is land that *they are responsible for*. Bringing Facilities in on the planning is the polite thing to do and you might find a lot of useful information about the infrastructure of your site. Site plans might reveal plumbing, electrical, or gas lines. If it is an urban school, you might find out that the substrate is fill from someplace else, and needs to be tested for lead or other contaminants.

Your school site likely has a landscape maintenance plan, which is orchestrated from a district office. It is important to consult the landscape crew in the planning phase of the project to ensure goodwill in the future. In our district, 160 or so sites are operating with reduced landscape staffing, so they are understandably concerned that a poorly planned school garden might be unsustainable in the long run, and a fallow garden project might eventually land in their lap. Providing the Facilities Department with a maintenance plan and a letter of support from the principal will send a clear message that yours is a coordinated, integrated, and well thought-out plan.

By including, rather than excluding, our various facilities crews, they have been generous in helping our gardens with deliveries of compost and mulch, and hauling away refuse and trimmings when asked. Get to know your Facilities people who are as determined as you are to see their school sites as attractive and functional as possible. —ABS

While you are at it, this might be a good time to ask your school board members to rally around your project—and the more information they have, the more useful they may be in supporting your ideas. Remember that as a parent some access to the school board should be available to you. It is, after all, your children that they are serving. You might also schedule a meeting with the district superintendent to discuss ways the larger district might support these schoolyard transformations. Be sure to invite elected officials to visit your site to discuss successes and challenges.

CONDUCT A SITE INVENTORY

Conduct a site inventory by touring and observing the school site to gain an understanding of how the yards are currently being used. Create a rough map of your findings, based on how the yards function. This exercise will reveal which areas are relatively unused and might be potential garden areas. Have a clear understanding how the physical education program or other outdoor activities function to avoid space conflicts. Be sure to share these findings with the school staff and gather their ideas.

If your school garden will be a series of raised beds to grow vegetables, this relatively uncomplicated addition can be done without a lot of planning. However, we have found that undergoing a site inventory to fully understand how the school site is used–whether for play purposes, or for its overall greening potential, will be useful in the long run.

A key consideration is whether the garden or outdoor classroom will be available to students during recess or free time. Some gardens

A seamless transition between the garden and the recess yard.

are located in the schoolyards, allowing students' unstructured access during recess and providing the opportunity for such varied play as digging, bug hunting, and open-ended exploration. Other gardens that are set apart from the recess yards are used as more formal outdoor classrooms only. In most cases it is preferable to make the garden available to students during their recess so they can engage with the garden on their own terms, as well as in more structured class time. The garden will probably need adult supervision during recess, a concern that should be addressed with the school staff.

To convey the information about the site to a room full of community members, footprint maps of the school should be available for meetings. Maps can most often be obtained from your district's facilities department, but if unavailable, Google maps are a good substitute. Blueprint-sized maps produced by a plotter or other large-scale copying machines are useful when talking to a room full of people. Be sure to transfer your usage information from the rough map to this larger site map.

ADDRESS BROADER ENVIRONMENTAL CONCERNS ON THE SCHOOLYARD

Undertaking this schoolyard site inventory provides an excellent opportunity to ask questions about some larger environmental concerns that may exist at your school. For example, are there enough trees for shade on the schoolyard? Do some classrooms need relief from afternoon sun to keep the classroom cool? Is there an opportunity to add a cistern for roof water catchment (which could be used to water a garden and conserve potable water)? Might there be an opportunity to improve rainwater percolation and reduce stormwater runoff on the schoolyard by removing asphalt? Could a solar panel on the schoolyard be used as teaching tool? A school garden might be part of overall ecological and environmental improvements, and a schoolyard that models sustainable ecological systems will foster a new generation of environmental stewards.

SCHOOLYARD TREES

Trees offer so much to the landscape. They can be a precious buffer between the schoolyard and busy city streets. They offer shade to students and teachers, and habitat to birds and insects. They may remind us of the changing seasons and can quickly become the center of a schoolyard. There are a few practical considerations, however, before you choose particular species of trees that will soften and enhance your schoolyard.

Fruit trees are a popular schoolyard addition; however there are some considerations before turning your asphalt into an orchard. Try to avoid trees with fruit that ripens in summer, unless you have a clear plan for harvesting the fruit before it falls. In our urban centers, rodents can be a problem, and falling fruit on a schoolyard will be hard for them to resist. Nobody likes to come back to school after summer break to a full-blown rodent problem. Apple trees, particularly the later ripening varieties, are a good option.

Deciduous trees might clog storm drains on the schoolyard during fall rains, so be sure to integrate leaf composting into your garden activities. Kids love to rake, so it shouldn't be too hard to collect piles of leaves for that important carbon source in the compost.

Be mindful to give your trees the best possible start. Proper staking, watering, and care for the first three years after planting will establish healthy specimens. It is thrilling to come back to a school site decades after the trees were planted to see a beautiful mature canopy that has sheltered countless organisms—including students.

NON-NEGOTIABLE SCHOOL GARDEN NEEDS

As you begin the process of imagining your school garden, please keep in mind the following elements that are essential to transforming an ordinary garden into an outdoor classroom:

Sunlight. The garden will need at least six hours of direct sunlight a day—eight hours would be better yet. Of course there are some plants that can grow in shade, but shade gardens grow so painfully slowly (lack of photosynthesis would be the culprit here) that they are unsuitable for school gardens. Shade gardens tend to be dark and sometimes dank places and we have never seen them work well. A school garden should be full of vigor and life, and of course the sun is the source of all that.

Gathering area. An effective school garden will need a gathering area that will accommodate an entire class. A gathering area can consist of benches, stools, hay bales, tree stumps, or anything else kids can sit on, arranged in a semicircle. Students will need to gather as a class to listen to instruction, complete a task, or to reflect as a whole at the end of a gardening session. This common seating area will immediately transform your school garden into an outdoor classroom. Teachers will feel more at home in their outdoor classroom if their students are not wandering around, and can be organized into one group. An outdoor chalkboard or dry erase board will make teachers even more at ease.

Pathways. The garden will need pathways to get through the garden. Make sure some of the paths are accessible by wheelchair. A class of twenty students should be able to navigate effortlessly through a space, and know intuitively where and where not to stand or walk. Clearly defined paths will keep the garden teachers sane by not having to remind students that they are standing in the wrong place. To make the space handicap accessible, some of the paths must have a hard packed surface such as asphalt or decomposed granite.

Tool shed. The garden will need a tool shed for storing tools and equipment. The tool shed can be multipurpose—it might also serve as the garden coordinator's "office," or become a focal point in the garden, displaying the children's tile mosaic artwork on an exterior wall, or support an outdoor workbench/potting station.

A sturdy tool shed.

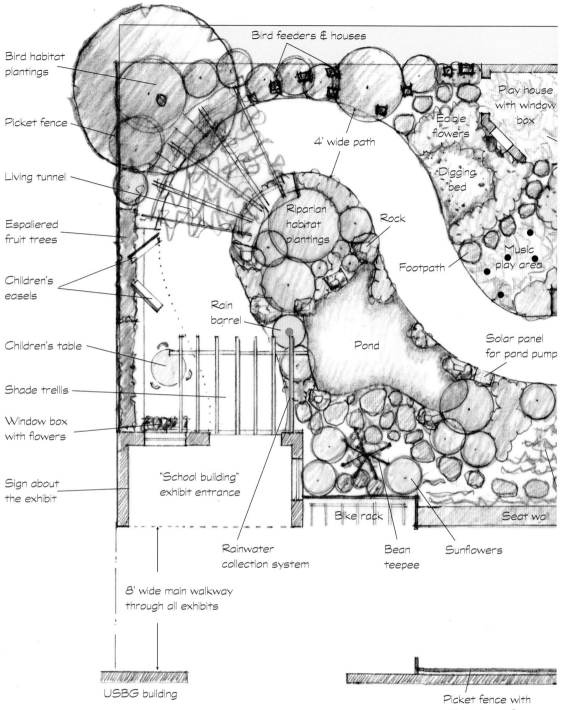

Bird habitat plantings

Picket fence

Living tunnel

Espaliered fruit trees

Children's easels

Children's table

Shade trellis

Window box with flowers

Sign about the exhibit

Bird feeders & houses

4' wide path

Play house with window box

Edible flowers

Digging bed

Riparian habitat plantings

Rock

Footpath

Music play area

Rain barrel

Pond

Solar panel for pond pump

"School building" exhibit entrance

Rainwater collection system

Bike rack

Bean teepee

Sunflowers

Seat wall

8' wide main walkway through all exhibits

USBG building

Picket fence with children's sunflowers & garden photos

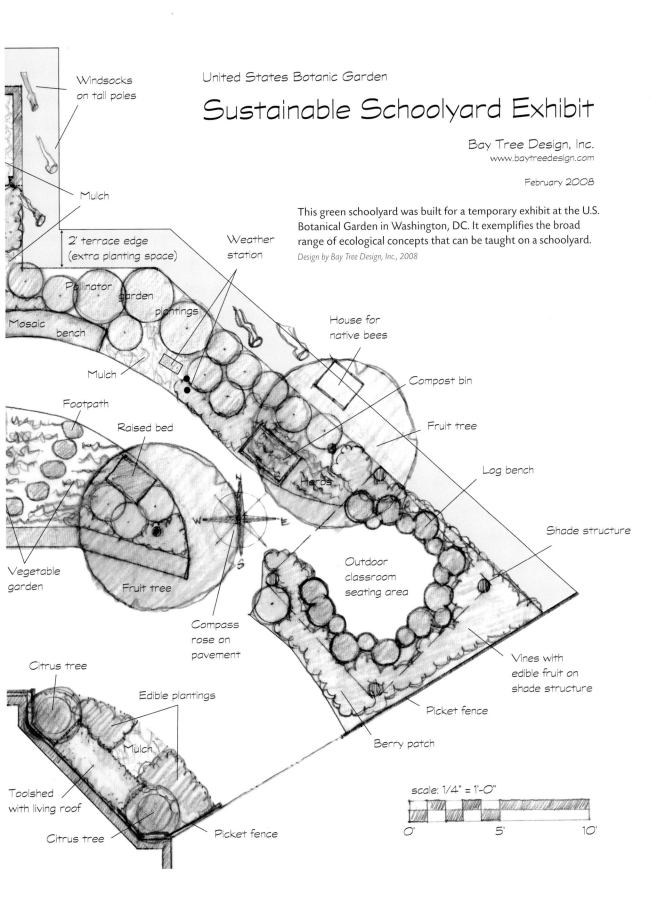

Windsocks on tall poles

Mulch

2' terrace edge (extra planting space)

Weather station

Pollinator garden plantings

Mosaic bench

Mulch

Footpath

Raised bed

Vegetable garden

Fruit tree

Compass rose on pavement

Citrus tree

Edible plantings

Mulch

Toolshed with living roof

Citrus tree

Picket fence

Herbs

Outdoor classroom seating area

House for native bees

Compost bin

Fruit tree

Log bench

Shade structure

Vines with edible fruit on shade structure

Picket fence

Berry patch

United States Botanic Garden

Sustainable Schoolyard Exhibit

Bay Tree Design, Inc.
www.baytreedesign.com

February 2008

This green schoolyard was built for a temporary exhibit at the U.S. Botanical Garden in Washington, DC. It exemplifies the broad range of ecological concepts that can be taught on a schoolyard.

Design by Bay Tree Design, Inc., 2008

scale: 1/4" = 1'-0"

0'   5'   10'

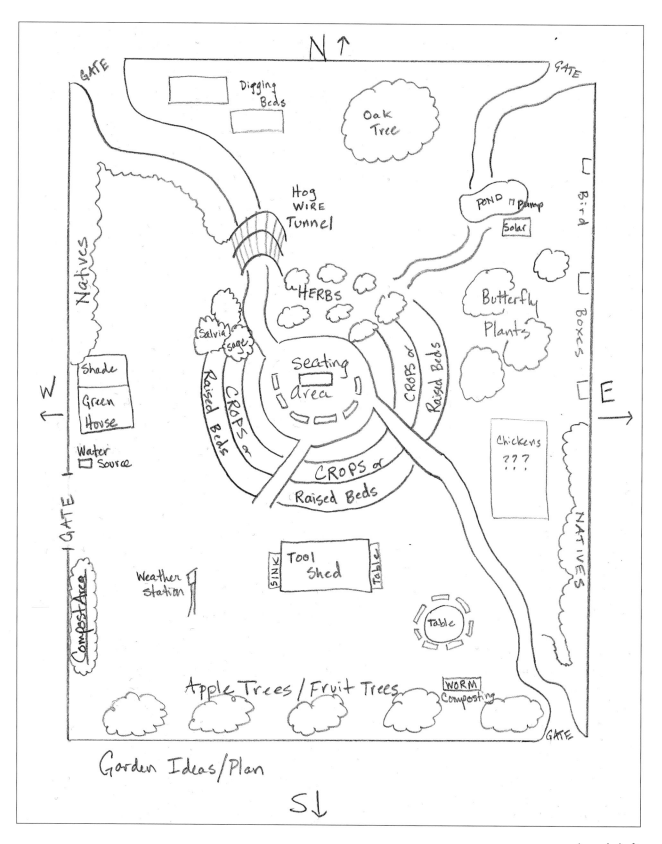

N ↑

GATE

Digging Beds

Oak Tree

GATE

Hog WIRE Tunnel

POND Pump

Solar

Bird

HERBS

Natives

Salvia

sage

Butterfly Plants

Boxes

Seating area

W ↑

Shade

Green House

Water Source

CROPS or Raised Beds

CROPS or Raised Beds

CROPS or Raised Beds

E →

Chickens ???

CROPS or Raised Beds

Compost Area | GATE

Weather Station

SINK Tool Shed Table

Table

NATIVES

Apple Trees / Fruit Trees

WORM Composting

GATE

Garden Ideas/Plan

S ↓

A rough draft.

Hose bibbs. The garden will need adequate hose bibbs, or outdoor faucets. It is useful to have several of them scattered around the garden as pulling hoses long distances is not fun. Watering is a pleasure for students, so don't rob them of their favorite job by installing automatic drip irrigation. While convenient for long vacation breaks when school is out of session, we have found that watering is a favorite activity for almost all age groups. It is also a basic garden task that students need to learn, as it will serve them a lifetime.

Good soil. You will need good soil in your school garden. Once you have decided on how your garden will be set up—with raised beds, in-ground plantings, borders, or whatever you can dream up, you will need to calculate the amendment to your soil. Amendment is anything you add to your soil to increase its fertility and tilth (the ability to support plant and root growth). The most likely amendment is compost. If you are taking up asphalt, there is likely to be four or more inches of gravel below it that will have to be removed to make it habitable for plants, so be prepared to bring in amendment and topsoil to fill the hole. The condition of the soil is an ongoing project; gardeners like to think that this year's soil is not nearly as good as next year's soil is going to be!

Fencing. You will need fencing around your school garden. Whether to keep kindergarteners in or balls and dogs out, a fence will define your project area and keep it safe. In our district, most fences are chain-link, which is not the most aesthetic option, but one that is durable, inexpensive, and easily available. Wooden frame fences with hog wire mesh have become a popular and more attractive option, however

Leonotis leonurus and *Salvia leucantha*.

wood requires maintenance down the line. Balls will probably find their way into the garden no matter how high the fence, so don't be too upset when a few plants are smashed; and no fence will keep out intruders set on getting in, so there is no point in making the garden look like a prison.

Plants. Once you have thought about where these elements will go, it is time to consider what plants to include in the garden. Food systems gardens are endlessly fascinating to students, and offer excellent lessons on nutrition and botany. Some schools prefer native plant gardens; some have great success with historical gardens. There is no end to the possibilities. We do recommend that you stick to plants that are hardy, can stand up to a bit of abuse, and are adapted to your particular climate.

Hopefully the garden will have lots of opportunity for expansion—and as your program develops and incorporates more classrooms, you will soon find yourself outgrowing your original space. We have seen gardens expand to accommodate greenhouses, more planting beds, an area for nature play, or a native planting area. Be sure to slowly and incrementally assume the maintenance of each expansion so that the school site will not be inundated by unforeseen maintenance.

DEVELOPING GARDEN DRAWINGS

Garden drawings may be as simple or as complicated as you want them to be. The most important element, however, is that they reflect a common set of clearly articulated goals and priorities, and that all stakeholders are involved and informed. You will want to start by mapping the information that you gathered by performing the site assessment, and be sure to include all the information that was gathered from teachers. Once the plans are drawn up and you have a design that reflects most everyone's intention, set up some time to hear the community's reactions. Communication can be very tricky, so be mindful that not everyone hears the same thing the same way.

One of the largest school gardens in San Francisco, Sherman Elementary School, had their garden drawings printed on a banner after their long planning process was complete. The banner was attached to the chain-link fence surrounding the school. It depicted the various facets of the garden—the pond and waterfall, the food system garden, the seating circle, and the native plant section. It was a colorful and easy-to-understand landscape plan. It alerted neighbors and pedestrians to the remarkable changes taking place on the formerly asphalt schoolyard. It was thrilling to watch the neighborhood become reinvested with their local public school as a result of this new garden.—ABS

This process of drawing garden plans varies depending on the size of the project, the complexity of the site, the resources available, and the pro bono talents of the school community. A visual representation of all the ideas you have gathered allows people to absorb a lot of information in a small amount of time, and will inspire others with the vision of the garden.

A garden plan furnishes the committee with a map to navigate the road ahead by establishing what goes where. A drawing of the intended project will be a great fundraising tool as the committee begins the work of raising money and awareness for the project—both internally, and in the larger community.

Many schools consult with a landscape architect or garden designer who will provide a rendering of the garden. These professional services have many benefits; ideally, they will ensure that the school is using the site to the best of its potential. Landscape architects come up with ideas you might not have thought of; are able to site the garden in relation to sun and wind patterns, drainage, and slope; and can help you plan the optimum paths of travel. Many landscape profession-

3. Getting The Most From Your Site

A living willow tunnel is a great feature in a school garden.

als understand the dynamics of institutional gardens—and specifically school gardens. Perhaps there is a landscape architect in the parent community of the school, or a local university has an urban planning and architectural department with students looking for projects.

We were to relocate our school garden to a steep slope on a sandy dune, which made for rather thorny problems. I imagined that we would pour concrete or build stone retaining walls to produce a series of descending level terraces, much like on the mountains of Peru. A parent knew an architect who loved this kind of challenge; so for a reduced fee, he came and developed a wonderful plan, which involved using the slope of the hillside rather than obliterating it. This was the best investment we ever made on the garden— and the beautiful plan he drew up helped us publicize the garden, garner support, and raise the funds to build and sustain it into the future.—ABS

STUDENT INPUT

One important group of constituents whose opinions should be gathered is, of course, the students. As with all aspects of an outdoor classroom, this inquiry can be tied directly to the curriculum. Ask the teachers to solicit opinions from their students. They might ask students to draw or describe in an art or writing assignment what, in their opinions, would be the perfect school garden. Students come up with remarkably interesting ideas. In addition to wanting a frog pond and lots of plants for butterflies, they may ask to include a rocket launching pad, a pasture for goats and horses (or unicorns, wouldn't you know), and most commonly, they will want a swimming pool. Bringing students into the process will build enthusiasm and excitement for the project.

FEATURES OF A FUNCTIONAL OUTDOOR CLASSROOM

As we've seen, an outdoor seating area where an entire class can gather will immediately transform your garden into an outdoor classroom. It provides a grounding area where the instructor may stand in front of the students and describe the activities for the class, or write instructions on an outdoor dry erase board or sturdy chalkboard. Some gardens have amphitheater type seating while others have inexpensive straw bales for groups of students to sit on. Whatever your material, configure it so that everyone faces forward and can focus on the instructor. A shade structure or rain shelter might also be necessary to protect the students from the elements. It is difficult for students to

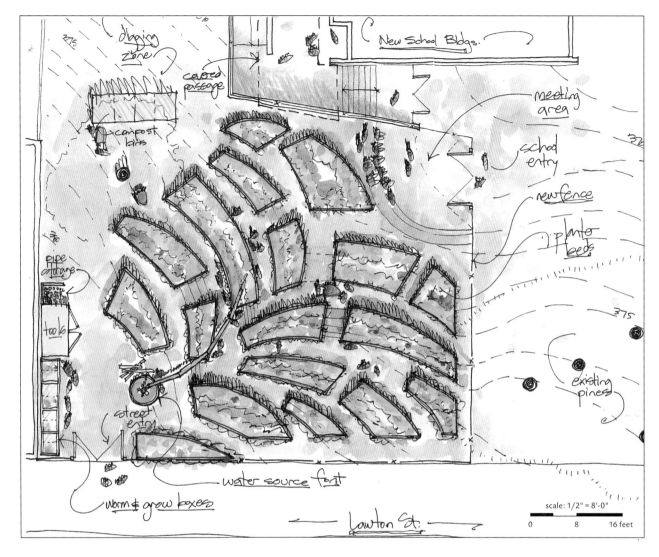

Labels within drawing:
digging zone
New School Bldgs.
caged passage
compost bins
meeting area
school entry
new fence
planter beds
pipe storage
tools
existing pines
street entry
worm & grow boxes
water source font
Lawton St.
scale: 1/2" = 8'-0"
0   8   16 feet

Professional garden drawings allow you to easily illustrate the many goals of your garden. Alice Fong Yu Alternative School children's garden planting terraces.

Drawing by Brian Laczko

concentrate when they are uncomfortable, so make this area pleasant to sit in.

We built our first outdoor seats with straw bales gathered after Halloween displays were disassembled at the various pumpkin patches around our city. We liked the ephemeral nature of the bales, and continued to replace them year after year. They cost around $6 each, so our annual "garden furniture" budget was about $36. The other added appeal is that we used the previous year's straw bales to mulch the beds over the summer. I enjoyed reminding the students that we were mulching with "garden furniture." Caveat! Don't get hay bales—they contain seed heads that will sprout oats and other grasses in your garden!—ABS

Another inexpensive seating option may be tree rounds. Be sure to find a variety that doesn't exude sap. Your local tree care service will be useful in locating trees that might be slated for removal. They might even cut the rounds for you. Baked goods are a wonderful way to thank people for this kind of pro bono service. For moveable seating, small stackable child-sized plastic stools have proven to be durable, portable by students, and useful.

A centrally located task table is a great place for students to do small tasks with their hands, like seed saving, cutting, or even drawing and observing with hand-held lenses. Ideally it should be large enough that a class of students can gather around it without having to jostle too much for a piece of the action. These outdoor tables can be built by carpentry-oriented parents and sealed or covered with oil cloth to protect them from the rain. If you have an electrical supply store nearby, the large wooden spools used to wrap electrical or telephone wire can be set on end and work as excellent (and free!) tables for a few years. Benches made of stone, wood, or concrete add pleasant resting spots for tired students (not to mention teachers and parents) and should be liberally scattered around the garden. Remember, tables should be scaled for children, not adults. If you are using already built tables, you can bury them in the ground to accommodate little frames.

PLANTING BEDS

There are many ways to design and build planting beds in a school garden. Your schoolyard will require its own unique strategies. Urban schools are often pressed for space and money, and container gardens are the easiest and most practical solution. Some schools may find they have ample space and are able to plant directly in the ground. Each school will determine its own strategy for bed design and pathways.

Raised beds

One clear advantage to raised beds is that they delineate garden space very neatly and help small children understand the difference between planted and un-planted space. It is a way to reduce the "no's and "don'ts." Raised beds insure that seedlings won't get trampled on when the teacher is not looking, and make it more likely that the *plants* will actually get watered. It is a simple task to install wire-mesh barriers to protect plants from marauding gophers. Raised beds also appeal to humans who like order and neatness, well-defined paths, and nature under "control." It also alleviates some maintenance concerns, such as weed control. Under some circumstances, raised beds are a great way to go.

Raised beds should be built to the scale of children—about 18–24 inches (45–60 cm) high and with a width of not more than about three feet (0.9 m), so that smaller kids can plant and reach the middle of the bed. You definitely do not want to build a raised bed that is too tall or wide for a child to reach into—otherwise they will climb in and compact all that lovely soil. If you are building raised beds on the ground, the bed needs no bottom and may be placed directly on dirt. This allows you to plant deep-rooted plants and ensures proper drainage. Be sure to remove any turf grasses and their rhizomes before installing it.

Raised beds built from wood are expensive to build, and resource intensive. In California, wooden raised beds are traditionally built from redwood, which has various rot-resistant properties, but comes from dwindling coastal forests. As we strive to model ecologically sensitive behavior, redwood is not a sustainable choice for building our boxes. Other lumber options might be untreated pine or fir, which doesn't last quite as long but is quite a bit less expensive, faster growing, and more abundant. Any lumber product in proximity to children's hands or used for growing food crops must be untreated. Although modern treated lumber no longer uses arsenic as a wood preservative, other chemicals infused in treated lumber are not suitable for use around children or food crops.

Many alternatives to wood can be used to construct raised beds. Some gardens use wattle (tubular netting filled with straw), which is

Straw-bale seating area and whiteboard for class instruction.

Raised beds do not have a bottom, but rest on soil.

EASILY NAVIGABLE PATHS

Managing many small students in a garden space is a challenge. and one can't even imagine the many situations in which one might have to say "no" and "don't." A garden should be a positive place to be, so designing it to work intuitively—without having to give a lot of direction—will avoid the following scenarios:

"NO! Mac! Please don't step on the carrot seedlings!"

"NO! Elaine! Water in the *bed*, not in your shoes!"

"Tyrone! The compost goes in the bed NOT on the path!"

Students will inevitably step on the freshly dug and well-aerated soil in planting areas from time to time. Take the time to design your garden with clearly laid out paths with an intuitive flow—around beds, up a slope, and to the tool shed or other commonly visited features. Go on a walk of the site and get a sense of how you move through the space, noting what comes easiest, and then refer to your notes when laying out the paths. If you are going to have raised beds, this will be easier than if you have in-ground planting areas. Well-defined planting beds (where plants grow) and paths (where feet go) will go along way in reducing the scenarios above.

(top) Well-planned pathways (mostly) tend to keep students out of the planting beds.

(bottom) Wattle beds are easy to construct and surprisingly durable.

Urbanite beds are virtually indestructible and are considered a green building material.

commonly incorporated to impede erosion on steep slopes. It looks like a fat straw sausage and can be laid on the ground in any shape and backfilled with soil for planting. It probably has to be replaced every few years, or restuffed with straw, but it is inexpensive and can be arranged to form nice low, rounded beds.

commonly incorporated to impede erosion on steep slopes. It looks like a fat straw sausage and can be laid on the ground in any shape and backfilled with soil for planting. It probably has to be replaced every few years, or restuffed with straw, but it is inexpensive and can be arranged to form nice low, rounded beds.

Urbanite, or chunks of broken up sidewalk concrete, either dry-stacked or mortared, has been used in recent years with great success for building raised beds. It is considered a green building material. Local Public Works departments might have urbanite available for free. In some cases, they might even deliver it to a schoolyard. Be aware, however, that concrete is very heavy, and use extreme care when moving it. You definitely do not want to blow out the backs of your parents on the first garden installation day!

The sandy slopes of San Francisco lend themselves to the use of bender board, which is a chocolate brown plastic 1 × 6 in. lumber made from recycled plastic milk jugs. It is not technically construction grade, but by pounding metal poles in to the sand, we have been able to build raised beds by strapping the plastic boards to the metal supports. While it is expensive to purchase, it is virtually indestructible and has not needed repairs for ten years.

Products that should not be used in a school garden:

✓ **Pressure treated lumber,** *as it contains chemicals unsuitable for food crops or proximity to students hands (and mouths)*

✓ **Plastic lumber made with wood fiber,** *which can be from pressure-treated lumber and will eventually break down in the soil*

✓ **Railroad ties** *because of their creosote content*

✓ *Old* **tires** *and products made from recycled tires as they may leach contaminants into the soil*

✓ *Most* **plywood,** *which contains adhesives (urea formaldehyde and phenol formaldehyde) known to be carcinogenic in high concentrations*

✓ **Recycled wood,** *if you don't know the origin*

✓ **Old bricks with paint** *on them to avoid possible lead contamination*

Also, before accepting a donation of **topsoil** *for a schoolyard, ask where it came from and what was nearby. Don't accept soil that used to be around the base of old buildings that might have been painted with lead paint, or near busy roads that had a lot of lead-heavy exhaust settling nearby.*

Adapted from "Green Schoolyard Materials List" by Bay Tree Design, Inc., produced for the San Francisco Unified School District

Container ideas:

- » *Recycled five-gallon plastic pots*
- » *Livestock water troughs*
- » *Wooden containers*
- » *Terra cotta pots*
- » *Old tubs or other retired recycled containers*

(right) Bender board is great for sandy soils.

(bottom) Roof-top container garden.

Livestock troughs are ready-made, durable, and large enough to accommodate deep roots. Be sure to drill drainage holes before filling.

Many school gardens begin as container gardens on the asphalt in the schoolyard. This is a great way to pilot a garden project and gauge teacher interest. In many urban school gardens, containers are the only garden option, and can be woven into a perfectly fine program. Planter boxes shouldn't be more than about three feet wide (0.9 m), so that smaller kids can plant and reach the middle of the box. Also, the boxes should not be so long as to be unwieldy and impossible to move. If planter boxes are to be placed on the schoolyard, they should have a sturdy bottom, drainage holes, and be raised an inch or so off the blacktop to drain properly. One difficulty with container gardens is that the plants in them are not unlike caged animals in the zoo. They are utterly dependent upon their human caretakers for food and water, as they have no ability to get it for themselves. If they dry out, or have insufficient nutrients in the soil, they will die. Trees are particularly fragile in this way. If their container dries out even just once, they will die very quickly.

There are many easy designs for building raised beds out of lumber. Several Web sites with this information have been included in Resources in the back of the book.

In-ground planting
In-ground planting is cheap and immediate, and gives a nice rural, farm field feeling. It requires few resources other than soil amendment

In-ground planting beds feel more like a farm.

and labor. The downside is that if kids need to take a shortcut through the carrot plot, they will. More work is generally involved in preparing the soil and weeds are a constant concern due to the reduced demarcation between beds and paths. In-ground planting offers the opportunity for students to dig, prepare the soil, add amendments, and savor the feeling of tired muscles and sweat on the brow.

With in-ground planting, weeds are quite a bit more difficult to manage, particularly if the garden is located where turf grasses once

A YEAR OF PLANNING THE GARDEN

September

» Pitch garden idea to principal.

» Develop garden committee.

» Research other school gardens in your area.

» Meet with school staff, committee members, parents, and other stakeholders to discuss goals and objectives of an outdoor classroom.

» Explore further fundraising options such as an annual fund, support from local businesses, or grant writing for foundation support.

October

» Ask for start-up funding from parent association.

» Find additional school partners to use the site (after-school programs, art classes).

» Conduct a site inventory.

» Map usage of space.

» Meet with a site plan in hand to discuss traffic patterns and current use of the schoolyard to determine possible sites for the garden.

November

» Ask students for their input.

» Continue to develop drawings.

» Consult a landscape architect.

» Contact school district facilities for support and site concerns such as, water lines, gas lines, or electrical boxes.

January

» Finish and approve drawings.

February and March:

» Develop budget for garden construction.

» Develop budget for garden program.

» Develop public relations materials for fundraising.

» Schedule a spring workday to prepare and clean up school grounds.

April and May

» Continue fundraising.

» Host an end-of-school party.

» Cultivate supporters for the groundbreaking in the fall.

September

» Celebrate groundbreaking!

were. Sheet mulching will suppress some of the rhizomes, but turf grasses are remarkably persistent and will require careful management for at least the first few years. It is useful, however, to have some school garden tasks that are always crying out for attention—like weeding—so successive classes will always have work to do when they come to the garden.

THE PERFECT TOOL SHED

A school garden tool shed must perform double-duty as a supply cabinet, and sometimes triple-duty as the garden coordinator's office. There must be enough tools and supplies to support the garden program, but not too many as to make the shed impossible to navigate. Ideally there will be vertical racks for long handled tools; a bucket or plastic milk crate with the proper number of trowels and cultivators to supply a class of about twenty students: proper storage for pruning and shearing tools: and shelving to house labeled plastic crates with school supplies, such as: pencils, markers, paper, clip boards, magnifying glasses, bug boxes, seeds, cooking supplies, etc. Ideally a teacher would be able to come outside with a class and their journals, and everything else necessary to make the class run smoothly would be readily available and easily locatable in the tool shed. However, there is a fine line between having enough supplies and having too many of them—tool sheds quickly fill up with stuff, so be very discerning about what goes on the shelves. Too much junk and you won't be able to find what you want.

Our favorite school garden tool shed has a small workspace and a stool for the garden coordinator to sit and fill out her curriculum binder. It has a rollup garage door and a bin of neatly stored supplies, seeds, paint for signs, and even has room for a row of garden books. A small cistern captures and stores rainwater from the roof. As if that isn't enough, the garden coordinator can use the neighbor's Wi-Fi for quick Internet searches!

If you have managed to stick with us this far, you have identified all the possible users of the new garden space, conducted an inventory of your schoolyard, and determined how a garden will improve it. You have invited all members of the school community and all levels of the district's administration to get on board and have developed drawings of your future school garden. Congratulations—you're ready to begin to transform the physical space! This is the moment most garden founders have been waiting for. After laying a year of groundwork, you are truly ready to build and sustain this project well into the future.

A school garden busy with activity.

Photo by Stephanie Ma

4.

GROUNDBREAKING, BUDGETING, AND FUNDRAISING

Congratulations! You have laid the groundwork for a school garden program and now it's time to put spade to earth and nail to lumber and install the actual space. A celebratory groundbreaking brings the entire community together no matter what size or type of garden you have envisioned for your school. Families will be eager to dig in, and you must harness and organize their energy to make the garden a reality. Set a date for the workday and make a plan that will keep all volunteer hands busy. Make an assessment of all one-time expenses and chart out how you will fulfill your project needs.

In this chapter we will discuss a few ways to ensure a smooth groundbreaking workday. Once the garden is in place, creating a rough yearly budget is a useful exercise that helps a school understand the ongoing needs of the garden. And to cover the cost of these expenses, you will need to do some fundraising. Later in the chapter we will show you what a yearly budget might look like for your garden program and how to seek out financial and in-kind support to cover budget items.

I hated to be a nag, but I felt like I had bothered just about everyone I had ever spoken to at our school to come help out with the garden groundbreaking. Many people said they would try to make it, but it was difficult to get a handle on how many were really coming. The garden committee was definitely coming, and I had the commitment of several construction-oriented parents. The day finally came, and we supplied big containers of coffee and tea, a huge donation from a local bakery, rented tools, all our building supplies, and a detailed plan of what we intended to accomplish. At 9 a.m. on the morning of the event, things didn't look good. Hardly anyone had arrived and to make matters worse, the fog rolled in and it was windy and cold and very bleak. By 10 a.m., we were wondering if we had advertised the wrong date, but suddenly, as if on cue, the fog lifted to reveal a bright sunny day and families started coming, and coming, and coming. We assembled groups of five to build and install sixteen beds, to plumb the garden, to establish borders, to dig a pond and install solar panels to run the pond pump. The kids were on hand to haul buckets of soil to fill the beds. By 5 p.m. we had accomplished a miracle, and the following Monday we started our garden program. —ABS

GROUNDBREAKING

The groundbreaking for your garden program is an event that requires a lot of initial planning. It is both a celebration and a workday, in which you will build both the community and the infrastructure of your garden program. Planning ahead will help to make the event a success.

Assessing your groundbreaking expenses

Understanding and articulating the financial needs of your groundbreaking will help you begin to find resources to support it. When developing a school garden from the ground up we suggest you budget for equipment, plants, community outreach, publicity, and possibly for professional services. This funding includes all one-time expenses to build your garden, and may include such tasks as removing asphalt,

INITIAL PROJECT MATERIALS

Equipment	Supplies and plant material	Publicity and outreach	Professional services
Tools (shovels, rakes, hoes, gloves, trowels, hoses)	Plants	Banners	Asphalt removal
Lumber	Trees and tree stakes	Flyers	Landscape professional
Heavy machinery rental	Seedlings	Mailings	Plumber
Debris-box rental	Seeds	Celebration supplies	Carpenter
	Gopher baskets		
	Compost		
	Soil		
	Hardware		

Raising funds—gotta start somewhere!

installing water lines, purchasing tools, costs associated with publicizing your project, and the fees for a landscape professional. Local businesses might prefer to donate in-kind services, so be sure to know exactly what to ask for. Parents will be your most responsive resource, so develop an effective strategy of outreach. Many schools use a visual aid such as a fundraising "thermometer," which visually communicates the resources raised to date. Publicize the project needs in the school newspaper or bulletin and be sure to inventory the skills of your parents.

Planning for the workday

Any work that requires the use of heavy machinery (excavator or jackhammer) should be done in advance of the groundbreaking workday.

Refer to your garden design and prioritize the jobs that need to be accomplished by breaking them down into smaller projects such as installing a seating area, constructing raised beds, planting trees or border plants, or bringing in new soil. Creating a loose schedule for the day is useful when coordinating multiple tasks with many volunteers of differing skill levels.

Each smaller project within your groundbreaking plan will require specific materials. Determine how much and what kind of lumber or other building material, piping, nails, fasteners, and soil are needed and have these items delivered to the site in advance of the workday. Place the appropriate materials in the space where they will be built or used. Ask your parent community to bring hammers, saws, post-hole diggers, spades, and other tools; and remind them to bring a pair of gloves. Some tools can be purchased as supplies to remain in the garden such as a spade or two, rakes, and a wide push broom. Be sure to plan for needed horticultural supplies as well; purchase plants that you intend to put in the ground during the workday. Calculate how many cubic yards of soil are needed and have it delivered to the site in advance. (For guidance, a quick Internet search will yield several links to cubic yard calculators.)

Delegating tasks

Certain parts of your garden design will require a skilled project leader to coordinate and complete construction. Find members of the school community who can lead projects such as building the raised beds, constructing the tool shed or greenhouse, plumbing, or planting trees. Other volunteers will be the worker bees helping to assemble the pieces, dig the holes, and fill the beds with soil.

The excitement surrounding a groundbreaking will draw a lot of willing workers from the school community. Don't forget to include the students—especially those who need to fulfill the school's community service requirements. Think of projects for younger volunteers, such as helping to move soil from the delivered pile to the beds, or mulching the paths. Delegate recruitment efforts among your garden committee members: advertise the groundbreaking in the school newsletter, on a school bulletin board, on the Web site, and recruit parents individually for certain tasks. One person from your garden committee should keep track of the overall schedule and be in charge of triage, directing volunteers as they show up and fetching unanticipated supplies. Be on the lookout for volunteers in need of a job. There is nothing worse than arriving for a workday only to find that all the tools are being used and there is nothing to do.

Skilled project leaders are a must for a successful groundbreaking. *Photo by Jen Thacher*

A busy volunteer is a happy volunteer.

Photo by Jen Thacher

Planning for the celebration

A groundbreaking is not only about the work needed to build your garden, but about celebrating it. Assign a committee member or parent volunteer to be in charge of simple decorations and fun activities or tasks for the children, as well as organizing food and refreshments.

The groundbreaking workday will last several hours and the work can be strenuous. Keep your volunteers well fueled with hearty snacks and drinks. Homemade goodies brought potluck-style are always better received than the more convenient processed variety. Taking the time to provide delicious home made food will create happy volunteers who will be more willing to return for future workdays. Healthy, homemade, nutritious snacks also set the tone for your garden program's approach to nutrition: eat well to fuel an active body.

BUDGETING FOR A GARDEN PROGRAM

Now that your garden is in place and the up-front costs of construction materials and the purchase of a few tools have been accounted for, it is wise to take a closer look at what ongoing expenditures your garden will incur. Create a yearly budget to present to the parent association to ensure that program costs are understood. Budget items might include a garden educator's stipend, tools, repairs to infrastructure, cooking supplies, and classroom supplies such as new pencils and clipboards. To create an accurate budget, over the course of the first year take good notes and account for all receipts for each category of expenditure. Once you've established a total for a yearly budget it will be clear how much fundraising will be required to support your program as you move forward.

Garden educator stipend

A garden educator often proves to be an indispensable piece of the puzzle, solidifying your garden program into an integrated whole. This position is frequently part-time, though sometimes schools find ways to bring someone on as a full-time garden instructor. Otherwise, hours can be filled out by additional work at the school if your administrator is clever. Depending on the breadth of your garden program and the schedule of classes in the garden, the garden educator might be at school two, three, or even five times a week leading lessons. There are many ways to determine compensation. Set a daily rate for each day spent in the garden or determine an hourly rate that is fair and within your means. Be sure to plan for a slight increase each year.

When I began teaching as a garden educator, my salary was $100 a day for 180 days of instruction. I was in the garden five afternoons a week: overseeing the lunch hour at noon until 3:30 p.m. when school was out. Each day I led three forty-five minute classes, with the exception of kindergarten day, in which the sessions only lasted thirty minutes; on Fridays I had one class each of fourth and fifth graders. Regardless of my schedule, I often stayed later to prep for the next day's lessons. I made $18,000 a year, before taxes. The principal at my school was sympathetic; she happened to need a literacy coach in the mornings and hired me in good faith that I could at least muddle my way through kindergarten and first grade phonemics. I found that I got to know the teachers and students on a deeper level than I would have simply through the garden program. I also gained valuable experience with curriculum and an awareness of child development that informed my teaching in the garden. After combining the literacy and garden work at the school I had a relatively normal eight-hour workday. Some years I continued to extend my hours at various after-school programs and even a solar company that one of the parents at the school owned. All told, I made a decent living and loved what I did to earn it. —RKP

Repairs and tool replacement

Every year there will inevitably be a few repairs that will demand attention in the garden. Solar panels get stolen and the pond pump no long longer works; the roof of the shed gets damaged in a violent windstorm; the hose is cracked and worn and starting to leak. Whatever the case may be, plan for these repairs and upgrades as infrastructure ages.

A bucket of trowels and digging forks (cultivators) will be used frequently in class and in your digging area during lunchtime or in other instances of free play. Some will get lost; others will become mallets, busting open old pinecones, seeds, and other objects. Eventually they will fall apart, get lost in the garden beds, or break—so plan on replacing them every couple of years. (Larger tools can last many years if they are cared for properly.)

Infrastructure improvements

Many improvements to garden infrastructure will be required over the years and planning for these projects is wise. You may decide that your initial prefab metal garden shed no longer works and your program needs a more solid and spacious place for tools and supplies. You might have your eye on an area of your schoolyard that you want to expand into and create a native demonstration garden as a tool for teaching certain standards. The center table in the garden has become a slide as

Human capital can solve even the biggest garden problems, and schools can tap into that bottomless supply of energy with a little bit of organization.

Teachers and principals learning Organic Gardening 101.

two of the legs have finally rotted through. It's time for a new, bigger table that all the students can fit around during a demonstration. Often if lumber can be provided, parents are happy to provide the construction know-how and labor. Set aside funds each year to cover the costs of these sorts of improvements, as they will inevitably arise.

Curriculum and library upgrades

Eventually the garden curriculum you use will be revised and published in a new edition. Your program should continue to upgrade along with the revisions when possible. You may also wish to purchase different curricula or expand your garden library with new children's books. While not a yearly expense, these occasional upgrades should be accounted for somewhere in your budget.

Professional development

Invest in your garden program by training teachers how to use and feel comfortable in an outdoor classroom. Garden and ecology-centered professional development for members of your school community has many benefits. Perhaps there is a local ecology center or science museum that offers courses in natural science or plant science. Find your local Master Gardener program or cooperative extension and look into what classes they offer. Likewise your local community college or university might hold courses in environmental science and horticulture. Fees for these trainings can vary, but be sure to devote a portion of your budget to this very important investment.

A YEARLY GARDEN BUDGET

Garden coordinator
stipend.................. $15,000

Repairs*..................... $500

Tool replacement* $200

Infrastructure
improvements*.. $1,000–5,000

Cooking supplies $100

Party supplies............... $500

Curriculum and
library upgrades*.......... $250

Classroom supplies........ $100

Professional development
for garden coordinator
and teachers.............. $1,500

Labor....................... FREE

*not necessary every year

Here in San Francisco we are fortunate to have a professional develop-ment program devoted entirely to school gardens. In Sonoma County, the Occidental Arts and Ecology Center holds three residential School Garden Teacher Trainings each summer for schools in the Bay Area and beyond. During this five-day day course, teacher teams learn about soil care, organic gardening, seed saving, curriculum links, and how and what to cook with students. Teams are able to strategize about their school's garden program and make goals for the upcoming year. Each participant pays $500 for the week; food and lodging are included. —RKP

Supplies

As in every classroom, supplies of pencils, erasers, journals, crayons, paint, and colored pencils need to be replenished each year in the garden. Keep track of receipts. Add these expenses to your yearly budget leaving room for unforeseen supplies that you might need for a new lesson or activity.

Many of the cooking supplies for staging a garden harvest feast will also need to be replenished throughout the year. Perishables such as olive oil, salt, pepper, vinegar, soy sauce, and honey are consumed quickly. Paper trays and dish soap should be restocked each year. Keep track of what is spent and include "cooking supplies" as an item in your budget.

An annual spring garden party is a great way to acknowledge your volunteers and to relax and enjoy the garden as a community. You will need food and drinks (though some can be brought by parents), plates and utensils, money to hire a band, and supplies for activities such as face painting, making sun prints, or making bird feeders. Keep track of what is spent and add this to your budget as an annual party expense. You will not regret devoting part of your funding to a party that builds community spirit; teachers can finally relax, parents can socialize, and kids can play and roam freely in the garden.

Labor

Each class provides at least twenty pairs of eager hands to help maintain the school garden. It is the students' job, not yours, to do the weeding, the mulching, the watering, the composting, and the harvesting. When you need more skilled help, parents will lend their hands.

Labor is in great supply in a school garden, with so many eager students wanting to help. The sweat equity that is created by enlisting the students and community in the maintenance of the garden will build a sense of ownership and pride in the school. Outside, skilled labor should be a rare expense, and contracted only after exhausting

the resources of your school community. You may choose to set aside a "rainy day" allocation for this and other unusual expenses.

Work gloves are useful for volunteers in the garden.

The first couple of years that I was a garden coordinator the parents would always remark "Wow—your garden looks so great!" I was oddly insulted by those remarks—it's not MY garden after all! The garden belongs to the students of this school—they do all the work of planting and watering and weeding and hauling and all I really do is guide and help them along. —ABS

All they need is a fresh vinaigrette.
Photo by Brooke Hieserich

FUNDRAISING FOR A GARDEN PROGRAM

We have seen over and over again that a charismatic garden program will find funding to support it. A well-run program and successful coordinator elevates the program; and the program, by virtue of its popularity attracts the funding to sustain it.

The most sustainable source of school garden funding comes directly from the school site. Special school district science funds, school site-council funding, principal discretionary funds, or parent association funds are common means of funding. Schools always benefit from an annual fund drive, which raises money to support the many school programs that are above and beyond the means of the school's yearly budget.

Succulents in old pairs of shoes—a small fundraiser?

Successful garden programs begin small and grow over time. One program that was started by a parent initially received only $2,000 of funding in their first year, but after eight years, had grown their annual fundraising revenue to $20,000. Having developed a meaningful and successful program, that founding parent secured funding over time for a paid garden coordinator position to sustain and continue to grow the program after her children graduated from the school.

Community investment

A school's community consists of several entities: neighbors who live near by, local businesses, local clubs, parents, school administrators, teachers, and students. A school garden is often the element that draws these sometimes disparate groups together, transforming a school into a community hub. Forge relationships with these neighborhood groups and businesses and encourage their support of the garden project through volunteer hours or perhaps in-kind or financial donations. A school garden will be sustained by many layers of support—be sure to cultivate your community to ensure a thriving garden program.

Organizing yearly workdays around the garden project is a great way to interest the surrounding community in the school and generate in-kind support for your garden program. We have had local coffee vendors donate pitchers of coffee, bakeries donate baked goods, nearby grocery stores donate lunch and juice, and local hardware stores donate seeds or tools. Local businesses have also donated professional services to a workday project—arborists, landscape designers, and irrigation specialists. Corporations often require their staff to take community service days; this is a great way to harness labor for big projects. Careful organization of a workday is key to its success, and it is a wonderful opportunity to draw in the neighborhood. Who doesn't want to help out their local public school? It is the job of the organizer to show them how and to provide them with an opportunity to do it.

Grant writing

Some school communities might have experienced grant writers among the parent community. Writing grants is an acquired skill, but with a little practice and confidence, it can be accomplished by anyone with a little time and some writing ability. Most public schools sites have nonprofit status (501c3) and are able to receive money from charitable foundations. Usually grants are disbursed through local, state, and federal government departments, or through private foundations. Large corporations often have foundations for grant making as well. These organizations have diverse goals and missions, and it is your first job to seek out the foundations that support the kind of work you are doing. Conduct an Internet search to identify local foundations that might have a similar vision as your garden program. Take the time to have a phone conversation with a program officer at the foundation. They will be able to tell you quickly whether or not your program is a good fit. If it is, the next step is to develop a proposal that you will submit to the foundation.

Successful grant writing efforts require programs that have strong leadership, demonstrated community support, a mission with clearly identified goals and objectives, the ability to communicate a vision, and a plan for sustainability. The act of writing a grant is useful for clarifying these topics in your own mind. Once a grant proposal is developed, it may be used as a template for proposals to other foundations. For more information on current grant opportunities, see Resources in the back of the book.

Most foundations have online application guidelines; follow them carefully. Pay close attention to how submittals are received and when they are due. Grants, like most things in life, are about building relationships. The organization that funds a garden program will often assume the role of a partner. They will want to be informed of successes and challenges, and mid-term and final reporting will keep them up-to-date.

As a rule, foundations prefer to fund *programs* rather than *salaries*, but someone needs to run the program, so salary may be embedded as a program cost. Start by trying to land small grants of $1,000–$5,000, and build as your garden program, and confidence, grows. If your proposal is declined by a foundation, don't give up. Keep writing proposals, honing your vision, and fostering community support.

There are many ways to raise funds for your garden program.

School site fundraising

A school should invest some of its own money to support the garden program. Grant officers will often look to see how much is being contributed to a project from within its own community. For some schools this is an easy undertaking. However, generating funds at many urban public schools can sometimes seem impossible. Start small. Begin by creating an annual fund for the garden. Ask each parent to give $5, or more if they are able. Create a tradition of giving each year, keeping your goal of 100 percent community participation in mind. Build on this investment with a walk-a-thon or an auction with donations from local businesses. Sell seed packets, made by students, and extra garden

School site fundraising ideas:

» Host a garden dinner night or harvest party and charge a small fee for entrance.

» Sell seeds collected from the garden and put into packets made by the students.

» Sell herbs from the garden, both dried and fresh, at school events.

» Divide roots and prepare cuttings from garden plants to cultivate, and later host a garden plant sale.

» Host a walk-a-thon, silent auction, or raffle with donations from parents or local businesses.

Movie night in the garden.

produce after school or at a school event. No matter how small or large the amount, some investment from the immediate community is necessary to build and ensure your program's financial sustainability.

As a garden coordinator I was asked to contribute an item or activity to the school's annual auction. Some teachers offered to take six students to a baseball game and out for ice cream. One teacher shared her crafting skills and offered to host five students at her house for tea and a necklace-making session. With the help of some parents I came up with a "garden movie night." I would bring dinner, warm beverages, and dessert to the garden and set up a projector. I offered to take ten students. Three families went in on the package, bidding against another group, and bought the movie night for $1,500. This was a good portion of the garden's yearly budget! I repeated the same activity for the next year's auction and the other group who lost out previously won the bidding.—RKP

Now that you've built the foundations of your garden, compiled a rough yearly budget, explored the possibility of hiring a garden coordinator, and gathered most of the supplies that you will need, what next? For the garden to become a real outdoor classroom, it must become a garden *program*. You've already discussed with the teachers how they envision using the garden, now it is time to dig deeper and figure out how to integrate the curriculum.

5.

DEVELOPING YOUR SCHOOL GARDEN PROGRAM

Now that you have a garden in your school, the next step—in case you haven't already started—is to develop a garden program around it. By locating curriculum to be used by teachers in the garden, scheduling regular classes, and providing reproducible and documented yearly lesson plans correlated with classroom learning, you will transform the garden into a garden program. Starting a school garden requires great commitment and organization, but without the program to sustain it, the garden becomes relegated to an "extracurricular activity"—students are not given an opportunity to develop a deep relationship with it, and inevitably interest in the project diminishes. The program, on the other hand, will provide students with opportunities to interface with the garden on a regular basis and invest no small measure of human energy to sustain it.

STARTING OUT

While the eventual goal is to involve all students and teachers in the school in the outdoor classroom, it is easier to begin a school garden program with just one grade level. To get the program up and running, a year of trial and error with one grade is easier to manage than with four or five different grades. This pilot year is a good opportunity to dig in with the most interested teachers who have self-identified by working with the committee on the garden plan. A pilot year also

allows the freedom to experiment and understand what is working and what is not. Year two might accommodate two grade levels, year three perhaps more.

Grades 1, 2, or 3 are ideal for a pilot project—second grade is my personal favorite. In my estimation, humanity is at its best in second grade, and the good humor, excitement, and enthusiasm of seven year olds is irrepressible. Seven-year-old girls will hold slugs and snails; seven-year-old boys will willingly eat new vegetables and declare them good.—ABS

Over and over again, we have seen garden programs grow by starting small, then expanding every year. Teachers will appreciate the infectious enthusiasm. Once they have seen the garden working, they will want to sign up and be part of a successful program. The lure of happy and engaged students is a strong one, and even the most recalcitrant teacher will find a way to use a well set-up and convenient outdoor classroom.

The job of coordinating an institutional garden for dozens of classes quickly becomes a complex management problem. As the project grows in popularity and more teachers clamor to use the outdoor classroom, the job usually requires a dedicated person to staff it. Very often, the parent who has spearheaded the project will step into the role of gar-

(far left) School gardens are outdoor classrooms.

(center) Garden coordinators are knowledgeable, passionate, and above all, organized.

(near left) The garden coordinator comes out of her house. (Just as young students think teachers live at school, they also think garden coordinators live in the tool shed.)

den coordinator once the garden project has been built. Occasionally, we work with a school that has a core group of teachers with the drive and capacity to organize themselves and run the garden program, but more commonly, a central person—a garden coordinator—is needed to make the program run smoothly. Sometimes garden coordinators are volunteers, in which case it is important to fill the position from year to year to keep the project from languishing.

GARDEN COORDINATORS

A garden coordinator, or garden educator (we use these titles interchangeably), functions much as the school librarian does, interfacing with all classes as they rotate in and out of the garden. Just as a school library needs a knowledgeable librarian to function smoothly, a school garden operates best when a designated person is in charge. Often this position begins with a volunteer parent, but over time funding may be allocated to support a paid staff person.

Parents in the school community make excellent garden coordinators, as they have a vested interest in the school and a personal knowledge and understanding of child behavior and age-appropriate lessons. However, we have recently seen a burgeoning interest by young college graduates in becoming garden coordinators. These young adults bring passionate energy and charisma to the school community.

JOB DESCRIPTION FOR GARDEN COORDINATOR

Ben Franklin Elementary School is seeking an environmental educator/garden coordinator for our new outdoor learning garden. The coordinator will work directly with students (kindergarten through fifth grade) and staff in the following capacities:

- » Planting and caring for a vegetable and native species garden with students
- » Developing gardening, composting, nutrition and outdoor-based projects in the outdoor learning garden
- » Acting as an on-site naturalist by becoming familiar with the garden resources and developing relationships with students and staff that stimulate observation and involvement in the outdoor setting
- » Supervising lunchtime garden visits

Responsibilities

- » Maintaining year round garden with seasonal vegetables
- » Working with school staff to purchase/develop garden curriculum connected to educational content standards
- » Overseeing maintenance of composting systems
- » Participating in ongoing documentation of student projects through photographs, transcriptions of students' words, and bulletin boards
- » Acting as a liaison between staff and parent garden committee
- » Assisting with grant writing and reporting
- » Organizing biannual community workdays
- » Organizing professional development for teachers
- » Making regular reports to principal, Parent Association, and Garden Committee

- » Coordinating occasional field trips and other off school-site activities
- » Supervising lunch period in garden
- » Mentoring new school gardens in the area and attend larger school garden network meetings

Required qualifications

- » Bachelor's degree
- » Experience with children ages 5–11
- » Experience in vegetable and basic landscape gardening
- » Flexible and creative approach to teaching
- » Ability to organize work and to function independently
- » Ability to work with students and staff from diverse cultural and linguistic backgrounds
- » Excellent writing skills and computer literacy

Hours and compensation

Part-time, $100 daily stipend for (20 hours/week) for 150 days of instruction (approximately $25/hour) Opportunities to fill out schedule at school may arise depending upon skills, interest, and availability Fresh produce

How to apply

Please send a cover letter and resume by e-mail to Margaret Bootz, Principal, Benjamin Franklin Elementary School (margaret.bootz@benfranklin. edu). Interviews will be conducted in late August.

A garden coordinator is a real advantage to a garden program, but funds are required to support this part-time position. Ideally, the parent association will fund the coordinator's stipend through their annual fund drive. Successful gardens that have existed for decades or more generally have this stable funding scenario, but your school may find other funding strategies to support the position. A garden coordinator is usually classified as a consultant and reports directly to the principal. The job of the garden committee is to support the garden coordinator by making sure that everything needed to run the program effectively is provided.

LINKING CONTENT STANDARDS TO GARDEN CURRICULUM

A successful school garden coordinator will primarily focus on teaching students in the garden. Many states or regions have developed a framework of content standards. They are designed to help define the knowledge, concepts, and skills that students should acquire at each grade level. Students are very often tested on these standards during the school year, and the resulting scores indicate whether the school or teacher is succeeding. Understandably, many school administrators and teachers are very concerned about ensuring that the content standards are met. The California Department of Education has published a set of content standards that we include as an example in the back of this book. Standards frameworks vary across states, regions, and most significantly, nations. Understanding your particular region's standards will help you make the case to your school community that the garden is a wonderful place to teach them.

Standards can often be easily researched on the Internet, along with many different garden curricula the amount and variety of which can be overwhelming. It might be easier to work backward by determining what the established curricular standards are for any given grade level, then finding a garden-based lesson that addresses that particular standard. Some states such as California have gone so far as to point teachers to specific curricula, by publishing the booklet *A Child's Garden of Standards*, which breaks down each content standard in each core subject and locates an appropriate garden-based lesson. Some garden curriculum programs such as Lifelab, Twigs, and others are available for purchase. Please refer to chapter 9, "Year-Round Garden Lessons and Activities," as well as Resources in the back of the book for lesson ideas and a more complete list of available curriculum.

Don't forget to look around to see what other school sites nearby may be doing. By gathering advice and perspective from coordinators who have already undergone the process of developing a garden program, you will save time and precious resources. Speaking to teachers, principals, and parents that have launched successful programs at other schools will also be helpful. Many coordinators have created their own lesson plans and are often willing to share them.

The table on the facing page, showing fourth grade garden program curriculum created by Nora Brereton for San Francisco's Koshland Park Community Learning Garden and John Muir Elementary School in 2009, illustrates the many ways to connect garden time to standards and lessons.

Working with classroom teachers

Classroom teachers keep a "scope and sequence" that details what units of study they will teach during the school year. At the beginning of the school year, the coordinator should meet with all teachers of the targeted grade level, and find out what units in their scope and sequence they would like to cover in the garden and when. It is important to let teachers know that garden time will be instructional time and to encourage them to work with the garden coordinator to develop ideas of what curricula to explore in the garden. Often a content standard will be introduced in the classroom, then echoed and underscored in the garden. Garden coordinators should use a lesson plan book to plan and record what is being taught in the garden, and document what lessons work and what don't for future reference. Regular feedback and communication with the classroom teachers will help to refine and adapt garden lessons.

Keeping records of what lessons and standards are taught in the garden, and maintaining a lesson plan book to document the activities will be useful for evaluations at the end of the school year. To keep the program vital and interesting, small adjustments should constantly be made. Yearly binders of the scope and sequence of education standards should have a place in the tool shed or principal's office and should be readily available for new garden coordinators.

Beyond curriculum: Making space for natural phenomena

While it is important to find relevant curriculum to build your garden program, don't overlook the unanticipated opportunities any natural space provides to inspire awe and wonder. A garden is a wonderful place for students to begin to understand something real about their own habitat, and eventually compare and contrast it with others. Despite the most rigorous intention to keep to the lesson plan,

CONNECTING THE GARDEN TO THE CURRICULUM

Week	Subject	Science standard	Lesson plan
1	First day: Garden rules and tools		Discuss expectations and consequences; get to know the garden and each other!
2	Compost and recycling	2.c. Decomposers recycle matter from dead plants and animals. 6.d. Conduct trials to test a prediction and draw conclusions.	Observe decomposers in our compost bins and soil. Bury different objects to test them for their ability to decompose.
3	Planting and seasons	3.b. In any particular environment, some plants or animals survive well, some less well, and others cannot survive at all	Refer to tables to decide what plants can survive well in our environment and what seasons they need to be planted in, then plant them.
4	All about water	5.c. Moving water erodes landforms by taking it away and depositing it elsewhere.	Simulate rain by watering the garden and investigate how soil preparation, tillage, and mulch affect erosion and water runoff.
5	Seeds and germination	6.b.c. Measure and estimate length; formulate and justify predictions based on cause-and-effect.	Plant seeds and make predictions on how they will grow; measure their progress.
6	Insects and animals	3.c. Plants depend on insects and animals for pollination and seed dispersal, and animals depend on plants for food and shelter.	Observe and record pollinators in the garden. Discuss different ways seeds are dispersed and make pretend seeds.
7	Native plants and farming	(Social Science) 4.2.1. Major nations of California Native Americans describe how they depend on, adapted to, and modified the physical environment by cultivation of the land.	Discuss diets of the Ohlone Native Americans. Identify and cultivate native plants in our garden.
8	Energy in the garden	2.a.b. Plants are the primary source of energy in food webs; producers and consumers are related and compete in food webs.	Create a food web together and diagram the food web of our garden.
9	Garden art	Flex/rainy day activity.	Make art from recycled and garden materials.
10	Origins of food	(Social science) 4.1.2. Mapping concepts, including: North and South Poles, the equator, prime meridian, tropics, and hemispheres; using coordinates to plot locations.	Plot where different food originated using a map of the world.
11	Soil and bed preparation	5.b. Natural processes, including: freezing, thawing, and the growth of roots, which cause rocks to break down into smaller pieces.	Investigate roots and water breaking down rocks and concrete in our garden; dig in the beds and break up the rocks that we find in the soil.
12	Last day and review		Say our good-byes and review what we've learned this season!

when something is really happening out there (and it almost always is) it is impossible not to direct our attention it. Our lesson plans have often been sidetracked by the remarkable natural phenomena occurring right in front of us. Seize these moments in the garden where the natural world takes over the teaching; students will not forget the time when a hawk dive-bombed the squirrel collecting nuts along the side of the school.

One spring we were able to watch a pocket gopher systematically go through a broccoli bed. We watched the plants tremble, lose mooring, and disappear into the ground like magic. Much later, when war was declared, I finally trapped (that is, trapped and killed) the awesome rodent, and with the fifth graders was able to examine its remarkable adaptations for life in the burrow: tiny vestigial eyes, digging claws, fur that goes forward and backward, and extravagantly lined cheek pouches. Many folks may not have the stomach for this kind of exploration, but it is a great opportunity to talk to kids about dealing fairly with the competition (trapping gophers requires a steep learning curve), adaptation, natural selection, and not to mention, safety.

I notice that kids who have been taught lessons in a garden are willing to explore on their own. After we have harvested seed from the nigella or calendula, I see kids picking apart flowers looking for hidden or developing seeds. While we may lose some of our garden's floral appeal to these inquisitive kids, I am always pleased to see their curiosity spill over into their private lives. Before you know it, they will be arriving to class with the odd pupae found on the sidewalk, a trapped daddy longlegs, or a praying mantis egg case. —ABS

Journaling

According to teacher evaluations, journaling is consistently their favorite activity in the garden. It strengthens writing and observation skills, and one can't help but be impressed by the progress a student will make over the course of a school year. Journals can be as simple as several folded sheets of paper stapled together, or can be inexpensive notebooks purchased at a school supply store. The covers should be made of sturdier paper so that they hold up over time. Every student who comes to the garden should have their own journal that travels to and from the garden with them. They can be stored in the classroom, handed out before garden class starts, and handed in when it is over.

A contemplative moment with a journal.
Photo by Jean Moshofsky-Butler

Journaling encourages students to articulate their observations. *1st grader, Alice Fong Yu Alternative School, San Francisco, California*

Plant Experiments

Predictions

no Water — It will be crooked

no sun — It will die.

no Air — It will shrink'n die

no soil — It will be

what really happened

no water — It is yellow and crooked and brown tiped.

no sun — slugs and black and yellow

no air — Black color change and dry.

no soil — crooked and black bit

MANAGING THE OUTDOOR CLASSROOM

The garden coordinator gathers the reins of garden management, guiding the classes as they perform the tasks necessary to keep the garden in top shape. The coordinator will also work with the garden committee to schedule one or two community workdays each year to build community support for the project and to accomplish larger, more complicated tasks that are beyond the ability of students, such as gate construction, fence repair, or plumbing improvement. The coordinator should keep a running list of all the improvements that will keep the garden running more smoothly and effectively.

An effective garden coordinator will lead the garden project while still allowing others to engage in a meaningful way. Occasionally a coordinator will be so excellent at the job, that teachers and parents are too willing to offload their responsibilities. While the coordinator will do the lion's share of teaching in the garden, keeping teachers interested and supporting them when they occasionally lead lessons in the garden is an important component of the program and will balance the workload on many shoulders. The underpinnings of a fully actualized garden program are the school staff, the parent committee, and a garden coordinator all bearing equal weight.

One of the first tasks of a garden coordinator will be to develop a weekly schedule of classes coming to the garden. On the following page is an example of a weekly garden schedule, listing grade levels for class time blocks as well as additional teachers and others who will be using the garden classroom.

Taking a class into the outdoors for the first time can be a wild ride. Initially, students are distracted by anything and everything—the scratchy straw they sit on, the mulch on the ground, and the drama of nature at their fingertips. They are drawn magnetically to dirt clods, to the mud around the pond, to the possibility of getting their hands on the hose to cool down their teacher and classmates. While a garden outing adds such excitement to a student's day, we strive for calm and focused behavior in an outdoor classroom.

The garden will always provide excitement and unanticipated surprises; however, the students will quickly learn to manage their own behavior as they become familiar with their garden project. Here are a few management hints that will make the classes run more smoothly and efficiently.

A WEEKLY GARDEN SCHEDULE

Garden schedule	First group	Second group	Third group	Lunch in the garden!
Monday 2nd grade	1:15–2:00 Jessie Brown Room 203	2:00–2:45 Susie Lam Room 202	2:45–3:30 Katherine Jones Room 201	3rd graders: 12:15–1:00
Tuesday 3rd grade	1:00–1:45 Mervin Wong: Room 306	1:45–2:30 Susanna Peters: Room 307	2:30–3:15 Josh Berger: Room 207	1st graders: 12:10–1:00
Wednesday Kindergarten	Kindergarten: 1:15–1:45 Raymond Ng: Room 101	Kindergarten: 1:45–2:15 Sabrina Maline: Room 104	Kindergarten: 2:15–2:45 Gina Smith: Room 103	4th and 5th graders: 12:00–12:40
Thursday 1st grade	1:15–1:55 Amy Greenspan: Room 105	1:55–2:35 Belinda Travers: Room 206	2:35–3:15 Calvin King: Room 102	2nd graders: 12:10–1:00
Friday 4th & 5th grade	1:15–2:00 Lila Joffery: Room 301 Kelly Nis: Room 305 (alternating weeks)		2:45–3:30 Eleanor Mack: Room 302 May Chu: Room 303 (alternating weeks)	Middle School: 12:10–12:40

Divide the class in two

Working with ten students is always easier than working with twenty, so whenever possible, break the class into an A group and a B group. If another adult is available, put that person in charge of one of the groups. While one group is learning about root structures and water uptake, the other group can be weeding the grasses out of the strawberries or searching for slugs and snails. A bell or whistle will indicate it is time to rotate groups. Having a menu of tasks that half the class can readily do without a lot of instruction or guidance is a handy way to manage a whole class at garden time.

Many gardens have a "digging pit" which is an area, bed, or box that is only used for digging—nothing has been planted in it so kids are able to dig with abandon and there are no worries about disturbing recently planted seeds or seedlings. This deceptively simple idea is a great way to keep half a class busy as the other half commands the attention of the teacher or garden coordinator. Children love to dig, and particularly younger kids find great joy in making holes. Some digging pits are strewn with fossils and interesting rocks and gems, adding to the thrill of the hunt. It is a simple task to fill in the holes at the end of the class to prepare the digging pit for the next class. It is difficult to ignore the admonitions of the students "Don't TOUCH my hole. I will come back to finish it next garden class."

Danya was a particularly avid digger in the first grade. He embarked on a digging project and I couldn't pry him away from it when it was time to rotate. He was making great progress toward China, which seemed relevant to me as the school is a Chinese immersion school and he was learning to read, write, and speak Cantonese. At the end of the class time I glanced over and saw his heels sticking out of the hole—it was all that was left of him as he headed for the center of the earth. I pulled him out, shook off all the sand and was grateful that class time was only forty-five minutes or I might have lost him altogether.—ABS

Recruit parent volunteers

Whether you are a garden coordinator or a teacher, it is incredibly valuable to have another adult in the garden with you. Parents often assist teachers in the classroom, why not in the garden? Advertise the garden class schedule at parent meetings; and keep a list of potential volunteers and give them a schedule. Often a parent will sign up for a few hours on a specific day to support you and help with classroom management. Typically the parents who offer to volunteer in the outdoor classroom are well-versed in gardens, so make the most of their expertise. As a coordinator, be sure to reach out to incoming kindergarten parents and recruit them to volunteer in the garden. The younger students need extra supervision and their parents are often motivated to help out and get to know their new school.

PROMOTING THE GARDEN PROGRAM IN YOUR COMMUNITY

A school garden will create a hubbub of excitement. Students reluctant to respond to the standard dinner query "What did you do in school today?" will always have something interesting to say about garden class: "We ate baby chard sautéed in olive oil with garlic" or "We watched the black bird chicks get wet in the pond" or "We collected snails and looked at their breathing holes" or "We counted insects that came to the sunflowers."

Art in the garden. *Photo by Ayesha Ercelawn*

Mucking around in the garden pond.

Besides this informative feedback that students will take home to their families, there is great value in keeping parents directly informed about what is happening in the garden. Many schools have a monthly newspaper or bulletin, and an article about the garden will continue to inform and interest parents. Weekly folders might contain a recipe for cooking with a seasonal vegetable. Dedicate a centrally located bulletin board in the school hallways for posting photos, journal entries, and student artwork reflecting learning in the garden. Keeping the material fresh and inspired will continue to draw in parent advocates.

A school garden has so many opportunities to integrate with a school day. We suggest taking a good look at the existing programs, and find ways to integrate. Art in the garden is particularly effective as the natural world provides so many sources of inspiration to teachers and students. Fabulous art projects such as murals or ceramic projects arise from experiences in a school garden. Poetry about particular plants or flowers also seems to flow more naturally. Does your school have a science fair? What about a music program? Could students take library books to the garden to read? Could you have a book drive to increase the garden-related books in the library? What about the after-school program? Might they like to use the garden? Middle school students may perform their community service in a garden, particularly when the garden is well established, and they have been

Garden Notes

This spell of warm dry weather has brought on some stirrings of spring. Our calendula and nasturtiums are blooming, the oxalis is burgeoning and the soil is drying out. It seems strange to be watering this time of year, but the rains have been irregular enough to warrant it. Hopefully we'll have some rain before the dry season hits in earnest.

The garden has some new and very agreeable improvements, namely the new drinking fountain by the digging pits. It works like a charm, and delivers a gentle, gulp-able flow. Our last fountain had fire-hose strength, which alternately bruised your tonsils or washed your face. If a child turned it on with dirty fingers, sand jammed the off mechanism and it was known to dribble for days. Thanks to Greg Kennedy (Grace, 2nd grade) for installing our new one for us. It is a great improvement.

Another modification is that the garden is now open for lunchtime and kids are using it with great enthusiasm. They march up with Samantha and their lunches and sit on the straw or somewhere in the sun to eat. Samantha is impressed with their knowledge of the garden, where to find things, and how to put them away. Most popular of course are the digging pits, which become the Egyptian pyramids, San Francisco complete with Twin Peaks and Lombard Street, hapless Jamestown before (and after) the flood, streambeds, canyons, tunnels—all in the course of a week. Thanks to Liana for finding the funding to hire someone to supervise it.

The second graders impressed me yesterday with their math and geometry skills. They were calculating the perimeter of each garden bed with little plastic rulers. I was surprised that they didn't really understand that each ruler was a foot long, and that it's easier to count by feet than by inches. Instead, they just counted by 12s all the way into the 500s. What nimble little minds!

Cabbage heads are ready to eat, so I guess we'll have to make some coleslaw. Salad is heading nicely; the radishes are red and round, ready to be spat out by those tender little kid-mouths unaccustomed to their sharpness. Sugar snap peas are just about done; only the most persevering student can still find them. Carrots have tall feathery tops, and kale is ready to cook. Best of all, the fava beans are stout and strong, promising an early spring harvest. All the students know to peel them once, peel them twice (pod, then seed coat), then cook them in a little butter for a delicious meal.

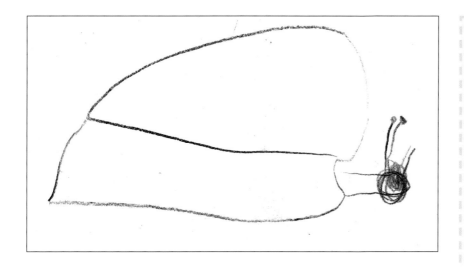

Promoting the garden program:

✓ *Write a monthly newsletter.*

✓ *Publish recipes using garden vegetables.*

✓ *Send home notes in weekly folder.*

✓ *Arrange an interview with a local paper or TV station.*

✓ *Take over a centrally-located bulletin board and post student work and photos.*

✓ *Have a garden party!*

Student art is irresistible—post it on a school bulletin board. *Keana, pre-K, Tule Elk Park Child Development Center, San Francisco, California. Photo by Ayesha Ercelawn*

using it for their elementary years. Other natural fits for the garden are cooking classes, nutrition education, and lunchtime. Students find the garden a relaxing place to eat a home lunch or school lunch, out of the fray of recess. Before long, the garden will be integrated into so many aspects of a school day that it will indeed become a beloved and well-supported part of the school.

TAKING IT TO THE NEXT LEVEL

A school garden is a springboard into the greater ecology and ecosystems of your neighborhood, city, state, country, and planet. When students recognize some of the natural systems that support the school garden, they will be able to identify them on an increasingly larger scale. Neighborhood parks, open space, and natural history museums are logical allies of school gardens. We have found that fourth and fifth graders are particularly interested in expanding their experience by venturing out on field trips beyond their school gardens. A small school garden pond could lay the groundwork for the study of larger, more complex city lakes. A school garden that grows food might inspire a trip to a local farm. Botanical gardens will amplify and expand the knowledge gained in a school garden. If this is impractical, visiting scientists are usually delighted to come to a school garden to make presentations to students.

Professional development

Teachers, garden coordinators, and parents will be inspired by ongoing professional development or garden-related training sessions. Check with your local university, community college, or community gardening organizations for a listing of garden or environmental education

Teachers examine nitrogen-fixing nodules. *Photo by Paige Green*

Local experts can expand your garden program.

classes. Teachers often are tired at the end of a school day but can be enticed to participate in an evening training when dinner is included. Summer is also a great time for teachers to pursue garden-based professional development, and helping teachers locate appropriate and effective trainings is helpful.

EVALUATING YOUR PROGRAM

As the year winds down, a careful evaluation of the program during the past school year will help you build on what works in the outdoor classroom, and rethink what doesn't. Ask all teachers who participated in the program to fill out a carefully crafted evaluation form. Try to ask questions that can't just be answered with a simple yes or no. If teachers can't find time to fill out an evaluation form, schedule a time to sit with them and debrief about the year. Evaluations over time are very valuable, and will help you guide your program so that it improves from year to year and solidly reflects the curriculum.

YEAR-END EVALUATION FORM

Dear Teachers,

Thank you for making this year's garden program such a rich experience for our students. To continue to improve upon what we do in the outdoor classroom, please take a moment to answer these few questions:

1. What lessons did you find particularly useful this year?

2. What lessons were not as useful? Why?

3. Would you like to have your own class bed next year?

4. Are there any new themes that you would like to see covered during garden time?

5. What aspects of garden class would you like to see more of? Journaling? Unstructured exploration? Drawing? Art? Others?

6. Do you have any thoughts on how we can improve the garden program?

Thank you again for your participation this year and for taking the time to carefully reflect on this past year's garden lessons and activities.

—The Garden Committee

Presentations in the outdoor classroom:

» *Beekeepers*

» *Bird biologists*

» *Pond ecologists*

» *Entomologists*

» *Nutritionists*

» *Local zoo-mobile*

» *Dairy farmers*

» *Poultry farmers*

» *Vegetable farmers*

» *Native bee specialists*

Tree dahlia (*Dahlia imperialis*). *Photo by Stephanie Ma*

Your project is no longer simply a garden—but indeed a garden program. It is grounded in curriculum, community support, enthusiasm from the school staff, and of course the contagious enthusiasm shown by students discovering and deepening their relationships with the natural world. There are many ways to grow a school garden. You will be the best judge of how to proceed within your community and make your garden project a continuing success.

6.

A HEALTHY OUTDOOR CLASSROOM

Some of the greatest pleasures of an outdoor classroom are the unanticipated creatures that will flock to the new habitat. Some are a joy to share the space with (hummingbirds and tree frogs). Others are more challenging to love (snails and earwigs) but we try to suspend judgment about whether they will be allowed to stay. There is never a need to use pesticides or other harsh chemicals in a school garden. We use organic methods to protect students from products that might harm their health, and also to model sustainable agricultural and gardening practices. We strive to keep our critter populations in balance in a school garden. When they do get out of control or when pests seem to be gaining the upper hand, we use it as an opportunity to teach the concept of ecological balance and to strategize with students on how to problem solve. You will quickly learn that a class of second graders is an enthusiastic labor force and can be as skillful as a flock of geese in plucking slugs and snails from a bed of broccoli seedlings.

School gardens are organic.

Our school garden had a "no squish" policy—students were not used to bugs and had no appreciation or fondness for them. Over the years, we studied the snails and their interesting hermaphroditic composition, their breathing holes, their sandpaper tongues and how to track them by following the silver slime trails. Initially, earwigs were deeply feared—those pincers, don't you know, and of course their reputation of seeking out ear holes to nest in

Aphid's Poem

Stephen 12/14/05

Aphids eat.
They have long feet.
They do not smell
sweet.

Did you know this? *Stephen, 2nd grade, Tule Elk Park Child Development Center, San Francisco, California. Photo by Ayesha Ercelawn*

- -

Searching for and investigating slugs and snails. *Photo by Stephanie Ma*

(they don't). But when female earwigs were found to be tending their nests of babies in the spring, well, they didn't seem so scary. As students became familiar with the natural history of the scores of interesting bugs and creatures in our garden, they found they no longer wanted to squish them.

The slugs and snails can become a problem pretty quickly in a school garden. The "no-squish" policy was in conflict with the buckets of them we would fill after each class. (It just didn't seem right to let them go in a neighbor's backyard—or in the park). But I soon discovered that a school family had chickens in their backyard, so during the snail and slug season, I would hand off a bucket to them each week and get a few dozen eggs in return.—ABS

Remember that a school garden doesn't need to be perfectly manicured, and a degree of untidiness with a kid-friendly aesthetic is to be expected and actually desired. Typically, some of the chard has leaf miners, the broccoli has cabbage looper holes, and the blackbirds are patrolling the newly planted pea bed for seeds. Rather than fret that the garden is imperfect or under siege, enjoy the fact that you have successfully invited interesting and different animals into your outdoor classroom to interact with your own species.

SOIL HEALTH: BUILDING YOUR GARDEN SOIL

Organic gardening is all about feeding the soil. In turn, the soil will return the favor by supporting your plants and making them happy and healthy. Good garden soil is the foundation upon which everything in a garden depends. You will know your soil is healthy when it smells good, holds a bit of moisture, and the plants you put in it are growing and producing healthy looking stems, leaves, flowers, and roots. In our experience, regular additions of high quality compost and a covering of mulch are convenient and easy ways to nurture the microorganisms that are largely responsible for good garden soil. These are ongoing garden jobs that students can be entirely responsible for.

Garden soil is made up mostly of minerals (those would be broken-down mountains) and organic matter. Organic matter is anything that was once alive: leaves, branches, animals, you name it. The organic matter is what feeds the inconceivably numerous tiny organisms, insects, and earthworms that live in good garden soil. You may not want to admit it, but these little critters are a gardener's best friend. They are neither beautiful nor charismatic, but they are incredibly useful and do us the wonderful favor of eating, digesting, and eliminating (decomposing) just about everything we put in the soil (except plastic perhaps).

Our job as organic gardeners is to feed these little fellas and make sure they are doing their jobs to the best of their ability. That means doing everything possible to make sure they are eating, pooping, making babies, and making little tiny tunnels through the soil. All this critter activity makes good soil structure, which refers to the way soil clumps together. Soil with good structure is crumbly and if you were to examine it very closely, it would have very tiny tunnels running through it (made by our critter friends). It holds water briefly, but drains, and is an ideal place for the roots of, say, your tomato plant to live.

Here are a few cardinal rules to keep your soil healthy:

1. Never dig the soil when it is wet

2. Find a good source of organic matter to add to the soil a couple times a year such as compost or well-rotted manure.

3. Do everything you can do to nurture the micro- and macroorganisms in your soil. You can do this by making sure the soil never completely dries out, or gets over-solarized by too much direct sun exposure. Several applications of mulch every year will help.

TWO HALVES DO NOT MAKE A WHOLE

Have you ever accidentally halved an earthworm with your shovel? No, the two halves won't go off and live happily ever after. The head half might live, but the other end certainly won't. If you are finding earthworms in your soil, chances are you have built it up to the point where it doesn't need to be turned any longer. By slicing through the soil with your shovel, you are destroying burrows, compacting soil structure, and generally wreaking havoc with your schoolyard biota.

As a legume, fava beans infuse the soil with nitrogen and are an excellent cover crop.

4. Once you have built up decent soil, try not to dig it or turn it over. Layering compost, mulch and other amendments is less work, and nicer to the critters working so hard to make your soil the best it can be.

Cover crops

If you have some time and would like to develop great soil, planting a cover crop such as bell beans, vetch, or rye grass will do wonders for your soil fertility and tilth. Any cover crop of the legume (pea or bean) family is a nitrogen fixer, which means that it takes naturally occurring nitrogen out of the air and fixes it onto tiny nodules on its roots. When the plant dies, or is dug back into the soil, the nitrogen is released. Nitrogen is a critical element for plant growth, and almost always needed in vegetable beds.

To plant a cover crop, students may seed the area, and water it occasionally. When the plants are mature, they should be shredded and lightly dug back into the soil. Students can shred the plants by hand or cut them up with scissors. We like to describe this process to the students as a crop that will feed the soil rather than us.

In a dry western climate, this is a great activity to do with students at the end of the school year or before a harsh winter sets in. In June we sever the plant at the level of the soil and shred the rest of the plant and lay it over the soil like mulch. During the summer the plant matter dries and decomposes, the roots die and decompose and release the nitrogen into the soil. When we return in September, the soil appears rested and ready to go to work. It is full of bugs and worms and our fall crops germinate and grow vigorously.

Compost

Compost is the magical secret ingredient that makes all garden soil hum with life and vigor. It is breakfast, lunch, and dinner for your soil critters. It has the organic matter that provides good soil tilth. Every school garden should have several compost alternatives: a worm composting box will take care of some of the green waste from school lunches, a three-bin composting system will take care of garden trimmings, and an outside source of good quality compost will take up the slack if you are unable to make as much as you need. In our experience, there is never enough compost.

A school garden would be remiss without a composting program, as decomposition is a large part of science curriculum in several grade levels. There are many resources available to help you decide which system is best for your school garden. Please refer to Resources for more composting information.

Our city of San Francisco has a very aggressive residential composting program, and each household has a green composting bin for all food scraps and garden waste. It is picked up in front of our houses and schools and trucked to the Central Valley where it is composted in gigantic windrows. We are fortunate to have well-established lunch composting programs in our schools, and in return we get large piles of finished compost for all the school gardens.

Vermicomposting

Vermicomposting (composting with worms) is an easy alternative to the more intensive, three-bin composting systems and can be done at school in all seasons. Red wigglers or red worms (*Lumbricus rubellus*) are commonly used in vermiculture and are different from the earthworms that you commonly find in soil. Red worms eat fruit peels, coffee grounds, tea bags, vegetables, crushed eggshells, grass clippings, and newspaper. Do not add bones, dairy products, meat, or bread as they will attract pests. Only sparingly add ingredients like citrus rinds, and avoid adding strong foods like garlic and onions. You are striving for a balanced pH level, and citrus will eventually make the soil environment too acidic. Food passes through the gut of the worms and is excreted as castings, rich in organic material and nutrients.

Lunchroom food scraps can be recycled in the school garden by a well-established, large-scale worm composting system. Or a small worm bin can recycle a modest amount of food waste collected from students who come to the garden during lunch. A worm bin can be fashioned out of many materials such as a wooden box with a lid or a large rubber tub with holes poked through it. There are also a number of worm bins available for purchase if you have funds to spare. Worms need bedding, and recycled newspaper shredded by many student hands is perfect. Other materials high in cellulose can be used as well, such as rice hulls or straw, so as to aerate the contents, giving the worms room to breathe. Shredded newspaper, slightly moistened, should also be added the top of a worm bin to suppress fruit flies.

When the food wastes are completely devoured, you should have a substance that looks, feels, and smells like soil. Harvest your worm castings by moving all of the finished castings in your worm bin to one side and begin adding new foods to the cleared area. The worms will eventually migrate to the fresh scraps and you will be able to scoop up the leftover castings. Some worms won't migrate soon enough and will need to be picked out of the castings you harvest, but students love this task.

Food waste that can be fed to worms.

Vermicomposting can be done on a small or large scale.

Most students will love their worms. Some students will be repulsed by the worm bin at first, but over time they will beg to feed the bin and hold a worm in their hand. There are countless lessons in vermicomposting. Explore worm anatomy with magnifying lenses, take a handful of unfinished compost and have students classify and record how many decomposers they find, observe whether worms will eat certain things like citrus peels, or a plastic spoon. Numerous resources are available to help you successfully set up a worm composting system in your school garden; see Resources for more information.

Manure

Manure is an excellent source of organic matter for your soil. Be sure that it is well-rotted and aged before it is applied, otherwise it will burn your plants. Horse manure is the best, followed by rabbit, cow, and finally poultry. We prefer horse manure in our San Francisco gardens because it is convenient—we have a stable in our city park that keeps it in a big convenient pile, and all we have to do is just go and fetch it. Cow manure is also acceptable, although take caution against getting manure from any livestock that might be receiving antibiotics. Aged rabbit manure is conveniently packaged in little pellets, and chicken manure is very high in nitrogen so a little goes a long way. Chicken manure, doesn't do much for the soil structure, but is good for vegetables requiring high amounts of nitrogen.

Students will chatter endlessly about manure, so be prepared. The older it is, the safer it is, and the less it looks and smells like . . . er, manure. When moving or handling it, be sure to have students wash up afterward.

Mulch

Keeping water in dry soil, such as that found in California or the Southwest, is always a challenge. Several inches of mulch on top of the planting beds helps to conserve water and keeps roots from drying out. Mulch is any covering on top of the soil; it can be river rocks, wood chips, straw, or anything else that will make a barrier between the elements above and the soil below. Tree care companies who do a lot of chipping often have a great plentiful supply of wood chips; usually they have to pay a tipping fee at the local dump to dispose of the chips, so are very happy to donate them to a school garden instead. Ask for clean chips, as they can quickly become contaminated with plastic and garbage. Be sure the chips don't have ivy or other invasive or noxious plant material that might cause problems; pine chips tend to work very well. The work of hauling and spreading mulch can be entirely carried out by students from as young as kindergarten. The work is fun and they enjoy it thoroughly.

Soil resuscitation

Many urban school gardens were formerly capped with asphalt. Dirt that has been trapped under impermeable surfacing such as asphalt or cement needs some serious resuscitation. All biological activity has been suspended, but with some help it can be brought back to life. Here are a few ideas on how to perform soil CPR.

Sheet mulching could be a remedy for lifeless soil if there's lots of lead time—six months to a year. By covering the dirt with sheets of flattened cardboard or layers of newspaper (to suppress weeds), then covering it generously with a layer of compost, then a layer of mulch, and watering it in and leaving it alone for a season will jumpstart the microbiology in the soil. The area should be kept moist, which will help break down the cardboard or newspaper. Sheet mulching will provide habitat for our beloved soil critters, feeding them a high-octane diet, and housing them in grand style (the mulch). This is a "build it and they will come" situation, so be prepared to watch as they multiply, and begin to breathe life back into the sterile soil as if by magic. We have seen sheet mulching work well on school gardens that were previously parking lots, asphalt yards, or playing fields that have fallen into disuse.

More commonly, when asphalt is removed, manufactured topsoil

This soil needs resuscitation.

will be brought in to speed along the project. Over time and with proper management, this will also begin to seethe with microorganisms. Soil is forgiving, and with just a little encouragement can become rich and loamy and extremely productive.

A schoolyard was removing a portion of asphalt. First came the saw, which cut up the asphalt, then came the hammer to break it up. Next a little excavator came to remove the chunks of blacktop and scrape up the layer of rock. Students flocked around the hole after the machinery had left. "Dirt!" they gasped. "Dirt is under the asphalt!" This was a minor epiphany. We just don't think enough about dirt. —ABS

Detecting possible contaminants

If there is concern that the school garden soil might be contaminated with lead or other toxins, send a sample to a soil lab for testing. This is relatively inexpensive and will put everyone's mind to rest. Several labs listed in Resources do this kind of work. Sometimes schoolyards

Students explore the drainage properties of different soils. *Photo by Stephanie Ma*

Living, thriving soil will be evident in your plants.

are elevated with fill from elsewhere, so if there is any question that it may be unhealthy, the best choice would be just to get it tested. If your test comes back positive for any contaminants, you have several options. To remediate responsibly, you would have to dispose of the contaminated soil in an appropriate hazardous waste facility, which can be expensive. Otherwise, you could cover the contaminated soil with thick layers of mulch and build raised beds for food plants. In the unlikely possibility of soil contamination, it would be advisable to contact an engineer familiar with this kind of work.

No-till or "lasagna "gardening

Nature teaches us many lessons, and maintaining soil fertility is vividly illustrated each fall. Think of the incredible carpet of leaves that covers our forests in autumn, and how that carpet, once broken down, fuels the miraculous unfurling of new leaves in the spring. This is soil building in its most basic form.

Soil is a miracle of roots, arthropods, mycelia, bacteria, and billions of microorganisms, only requiring protection from the sun, a

LASAGNA GARDENING WITH FOURTH GRADERS

The process of building layers on top of the soil rather than digging into the soil is called lasagna gardening by some, referring to the layering of materials. Others call it no-till gardening. Whatever you prefer to call it, it can easily be done by students of almost any age. In places with snowy winters, it is best to do this in the fall before snow is on the ground. In places with rainy winters, it may be done during the fall or winter. In a school garden, we layer the beds that will lie fallow for the summer. When we return in autumn, we have wonderful deep soil for planting.

1. Procure newspaper or flattened cardboard. Ask the students to layer it on the soil. This barrier will suppress weed growth. If you are using newspaper, wetting it first will keep it from flying around. You could also pin cardboard to the ground with landscape pins.

2. Have the students cover the cardboard or paper with about four inches of compost if you have it.

3. If not, you may layer it with whatever you have—peat moss, tree chips, grass clippings, weeds (that have not formed seed heads yet), shredded newspaper, pine needles, leaves, manure, coffee grounds, vegetable trimmings, plant clippings, seaweed, straw, etc. Help your students think of this layering as a horizontal compost pile, and maintain it as such. Layer the greens and browns as best as you can, keep it as moist as a wrung-out sponge, and don't worry over it too much.

4. It will take some time, but in a number of months, when the top layer is scraped aside and the black crumbly soil is revealed below, it is all one can do not to fall on one's knees in astonishment and awe.

5. Pick yourself up and plant your seedlings. Ask the students to "part" the soil with a trowel rather than dig it. Nestle the seedling roots into the slot, and prepare to watch them grow vigorously!

6. Continue to top dress the beds as needed, and continue to avoid slicing into the soil with any tools. These concepts can be readily explained to students.

bit of moisture, and some delicious biodegrading matter. By imitating Mother Nature and layering materials on top of the soil, you will support and foster all this miraculous life.

Slicing into soil with a shovel or spade is wildly disruptive to the millions of critters that live there. It would be the equivalent of a wrecking ball smashing into your house. Your hallway is destroyed, your kitchen is a mess of splinters and strewn appliances, and the roof is where the front door used to be. Think of this scenario the next time you are compelled to dig the soil.

ORGANIC PLANT HEALTH

There are a great many varieties of organic plant foods, but several are particularly suited to school gardens. We mention two methods that we find are easy and foolproof. Allow students the opportunity to follow directions, mix, and apply these fertilizers.

Fish emulsion

Fish emulsion is a very gentle fertilizer that is a must in school gardens. It is made of decomposed fish that is blended into a thick slurry. It is diluted with water and applied to the soil, although some people use it as a foliar feed by pouring it directly on the plant leaves.

Fish emulsion might just be the stinkiest thing known to mankind. It is appalling, and yet somehow fascinating. Watch as students recoil in horror from the smell of a watering can filled with fish emulsion solution. Then observe closely as they come back around for another whiff.

Compost tea

Have students partially fill a burlap bag with finished compost. This will be the "tea bag." Tie it off and put it in a plastic garbage can and fill it with water. After about a week the water will be a dark brown color, and your tea will have "steeped" long enough.

The tea is an excellent gentle fertilizer for young seedlings, and plants benefit from that extra little jolt of nutrition that it provides. What's left in the burlap bag may be dried and spread on the garden beds.

ORGANIC PEST CONTROL

There are many methods of organic pest control. We list a few here that are really effective, appropriate for school gardens, and that students can make by following a simple recipe.

Some pests can be used for explorations.
How can you make a snail go faster?
Photo by Stephanie Ma

Anti-fungal spray

Combine four cloves of crushed garlic and a tablespoon of mineral oil and mix. Let this sit overnight. Strain the garlic from the mixture and combine one pint of water with the oil in a spray bottle. Add a teaspoon of dish soap to the bottle and mix. This garlic spray is an insecticide as well as fungicide. Use it on plants that are overwhelmed with aphids or powdery mildew.

Insecticidal soap

Insecticidal soap has been around for centuries as a method for eliminating pests. It disrupts the membrane of soft-bodied insects and they die of dehydration. Use two tablespoons of liquid soap (not detergent) to one quart of water and put it in a spray bottle. Students can both make the soap solution as well as find and spray the infestation.

Sluggo

Sluggo is a slug and snail bait that is safe to use around pets and children and is considered an organic control. This product might be an appropriate defense during a summer or spring break while the populations are really ramping up. Otherwise, we recommend that students carry out most of your slug and snail control. They quickly learn where to find the little critters, and provide the most comprehensive assault on them.

Copper tape

Copper tape generates a small electrical charge when slugs and snails cross it. It can be useful to stop slugs and snails getting into plant pots or raised beds. It can be expensive, but is an effective way to protect seedlings, and students "get a charge" out of trying to coax their little mollusks over a strip of copper.

Biological control/Attracting beneficial insect predators

The insect world, like most of nature, is red in tooth and claw. The drama that occurs daily in the school garden between ladybug larvae and the aphids on the fava beans is better than most horror movies. Developing your insectaries, or plants that are likely to attract beneficial insects (or insects that eat common garden pests), will help build your dizzyingly complex and diverse insect communities.

Manual removal

Of course this is the most interesting and school-garden–friendly method of pest eradication. Enlist your students to find slugs, snail, cabbage loopers, aphids, earwigs, and soil grubs. Look at them with hand lenses, understand their biology, and at the end of class deposit them in a bowl. (You will take care of these critters in private.) We highly recommend this method for most pest problems.

KEEPING IT ORGANIC: STUDENTS AS STEWARDS OF THE GARDEN

In a school garden we have little use for efficiency. With sixty students coming out to the garden in a school day to learn lessons and do activities, the last thing we need is to cut corners to make less work. Students come to the garden, happy to pitch in and keep their school garden healthy and functioning at full capacity.

The ongoing tasks of weeding, watering, amending the soil, maintaining the tool supply, building and turning the compost pile, hauling, raking, sweeping, sieving, shoveling, planting, hoeing, mulching, sign making, and just about everything else except operating heavy machinery may be done by students. Even pruning, when carefully supervised, can be done with small groups of fifth graders. Student enthusiasm and energy will fuel the organic engine that drives the garden program.

Easy organic methods for a school garden:

Soil health

✓ *Cover crops*

✓ *Compost*

✓ *Manure*

Organic plant health

✓ *Anti-fungal spray*

✓ *Insecticidal soap*

✓ *Fish emulsion*

✓ *Compost tea*

Combating pests

✓ *Sluggo*

✓ *Copper tape*

✓ *Biological control (attracting beneficial insects)*

✓ *Manual removal*

A WORD ABOUT VANDALISM

School garden vandalism, while rare, does occur, particularly in our larger cities. Petty thieves force their way into tool sheds and usually only find ratty old trowels, cultivators, and other tools. There is rarely much of value in a school garden tool shed, but anything that is secured with a lock is tempting. Occasionally plantings will be damaged, and walls will be marked with graffiti, but this is just part of the urban landscape. When this happens, clean up the damage and replant quickly. Talk to the students about it, and ask for their reactions. After it is discussed, put it behind you and move on. If a series of incidents occurs, ask the neighborhood police to swing by on weekend nights and ask neighbors to keep a look out.

A WORD ABOUT SAFETY

It is not hard to be alarmed by the thought of twenty excited kindergarten students with sharp trowels clustered around a garden bed. Safety guidelines and common sense rules will help avoid accidents. Tool safety must be clearly taught from the beginning of a garden program, and meticulously enforced. Using tools is a privilege and students who don't follow the rules will lose that privilege. As the garden adult, model and insist upon careful and safe tool usage. Splitting the class into two groups and working with fewer students with tools at a time is a good, practical solution to avoiding safety concerns. An easily accessible first aid kit should be part of every tool shed.

Become familiar with your school's procedures for fire, earthquake, and other safety issues. It is likely that a safety drill might occur during a garden class. With your school administration, create specific garden procedures for these drills and practice them with each class that comes to the garden.

7.

TRICKS OF
THE TRADE

As a school garden matures, techniques and processes for running the program are honed and simplified. You are developing deeper relationships and communicating with the parent community. You are working closely with the teaching staff, and under your watchful guidance, the students are the primary stewards of the garden. You have discovered that many hands make light work and keeping all of them busy and purposeful is the key to meaningful garden sessions. As your garden ripens, you will discover various other efficient systems and helpful methods on your own. In this chapter we outline some of our own tricks of the trade. This knowledge comes from many years of trial and error, collaboration with other gardens, and research. It is further shaped by budgetary and time constraints that most anyone in school environments will be familiar with. We have organized these tips into the following categories: programmatic, class management, garden support, and maintenance.

PROGRAMMATIC TIPS

Running a garden program requires a great deal of organization as well as materials. Garden coordinators will inevitably accumulate books, curricula, school "procedure" binders, a walkie-talkie, and the other accoutrements of being a teacher and will need a place to house them. Carve out a place within the school such as a shelf or two in the library, or an extra desk in the school office, or any other free workspace to make into the garden office. A desk within the tool shed is the most ideal and convenient option as you can readily reference curriculum, scope and sequence binders, lesson plan books (see below), or the garden planting map can be referenced at a moment's notice. Confer with your principal and she will most likely help you find a place that works.

Develop a garden class schedule

The first few visits to the garden can be very exciting for the students, veering toward chaotic, so the more parent help available to manage the enthusiasm the better. Work with the teachers to develop a weekly garden class schedule. Once time slots are established for each class, encourage parents to come as a regular volunteer when their child is in the garden. A clear schedule of garden time and volunteer help will be very comforting to the teachers. It is very helpful for them to know that they have a designated time in the garden, say Tuesdays from 1:00 to 1:45, and that a parent, garden coordinator, or capable volunteer will accompany the class to the garden or be there when they arrive. This schedule should be as hard and fast as possible. The students quickly learn when their garden time is and they look forward to it. Let parents know when garden day is so they can remind their kids to wear their gardening clothes. We suggest scheduling one grade level per day, as this will help you focus on one set of standards at a time. It is hard to switch immediately from teaching kindergarteners to fifth graders.

Invest in a lesson plan book

A lesson plan book, a blank teacher's notebook for lesson planning with room for reflection and other notes, is an indispensable tool for a garden educator. Your school may provide them to you; if not, find your local education supply store and purchase one. There are numerous variations on this often soft-covered, spiral-bound booklet. Look for one that is formatted to proceed week-by-week, with plenty of note writing space. After meeting with the teacher teams to discern the scope and sequence of the curriculum, you can begin to roughly plan your weekly lessons. Write down your lesson plans and any notes on supplies you may need to gather. After each garden class go back to your book and record what actually happened, noting things to remember about what worked and what didn't. Having a complete record of your year in the garden will be extremely helpful as a reference for next year and for observing the progress of your program. Do not underestimate the importance of having this history to refer to.

When I started teaching in the garden the lesson plan books from the previous three years were passed on to me. I looked through each of them cover-to-cover and began to get a sense of the rhythms of the school year in the garden. I, of course, got my own matching lesson plan book and began roughly plotting out planting times, harvest times, and feast days. In and among these plant-driven duties I planned more academic lessons based on the teachers' sequence of units for the semester. I was determined to underscore, outdoors in the garden, what was being taught indoors. I did my best to record my thoughts on each lesson and to write down notes. I knew that the next time I would hold off on asking the first graders to write "decomposition" in their journals (they just weren't there yet). Instead, we would just draw what it looked like! —RKP

Train all students in basic garden tasks

Every student in the school should know basic garden skills such as weeding, watering, planting, harvesting, and cooking. Make it your mandate to have each class that comes to the garden learn these skills. You will rely on your students retaining this knowledge throughout the life of your program (and hopefully throughout their lives), entrusting them to accomplish these tasks without much supervision. Dividing the class into groups, sending one group to perform unsupervised jobs like weeding and watering, while lesson plans are carried out with the other, is a useful technique discussed in more detail in the section on classroom management tips.

Record student comments

When you've completed instruction and students are busy harvesting, watering, digging, or engaged in some other activity, take a moment to listen carefully to what they are saying to each other. Take out your pad of paper and record some of their comments, or hang a clipboard

Students are enthusiastic about using tools. *Photo by Brooke Hieserich*

and encourage the other teachers to include interesting and original comments overheard in their classes as well. Often these understated communications between classmates reveal their problem-solving processes, interests, and insights; they can also be hilarious! Use these comments in funding reports, evaluations of your program, and as a general record of anecdotes from the garden to share with parents and visitors.

Create competitions out of maintenance tasks

Make garden maintenance into a competition and it becomes both a lesson and a game for the students. Hand out extra carrots to those teams that pull the longest weed (have them measure it), collect the most garbage (have them weigh it), or collect the largest number of slugs and snails (have them graph it). Keep track of the benchmarks reached in each competition in the garden. From class to class and even from year to year students will demand to know if they have broken a record of any kind.

Create a cooking and outdoor kitchen tool kit

Keep a large rubber bin in the garden shed for cooking supplies. Maintain a supply of plates, utensils, cutting boards, knives, salt and pepper, and olive oil; and keep your salad spinner, wok, stove, and fuel in this bin as well. This kit will be indispensable when harvest day comes. More details on how to create these kitchen bins can be found in chapter 8, "Planting, Harvesting, and Cooking in the Garden," as well as in the recipe section in the back of the book.

Place tables and seats throughout the garden

Many lessons in the garden will require your students to do some writing. Clipboards serve as a handy mobile desk in the outdoor classroom. However, a project table for certain lessons and activities is indispensable as students need a stable surface and the ability to use both hands to perform delicate tasks such as seed saving or plant dissection. Besides having a large center staging table in the garden, consider building another table for an alternate gathering location, or scatter flat-topped benches throughout the garden. Students gravitate toward these spaces to convene, compare notes, and jot down answers to questions or problems.

Individual stools that students can take with them to their own space become indispensable when they are sketching or journaling in the garden. Stools are useful for independent study and quiet observation. They can be purchased inexpensively or fashioned from various materials. Stacking stools are often preferable for easy storage.

Model creative reuse of materials

Waste is a resource and a school garden is a perfect place to teach the creative reuse of products once doomed to the landfill. Used hard plastic sandwich containers make great bug habitats for individual students during their search for insects in the garden. Likewise, old boxes can be transformed into terrariums for butterfly hatchings. Dip mature pinecones in tahini or peanut butter, roll them in bird seed, and string them throughout the garden to attract various avian visitors. Collect worn-out dinnerware from families for a mosaic beautification project along a wall in the garden. Use recycled newspaper to feed your worm bin. Ask parents to bring in yogurt containers and plastic juice jugs for watering. Paint and plant old terra cotta pots as garden gifts. The garden should be a model of ecological stewardship: reduce, reuse, recycle, and rot!

Student interpretations of the garden are often revealing.
1st grader, Tule Elk Park Child Development Center, San Francisco, California. Photo by Ayesha Ercelawn

A skillful artist with student help can turn old ceramics into inspired mosaics.

CLASS MANAGEMENT TIPS

Young students are particularly excited about coming to the garden. Have them develop the habit of settling down a little bit before they come through the garden gate. Remind them that they are entering another world, and ask them to use all their senses to experience the garden. Ask them to use their eyes, ears, and noses to detect differences in the environment. When they arrive at the gathering area, ask for their impressions. Listen carefully and thank them for their participation.

Remind students that even though they are outside, it is not recess time. Keeping young students (kindergarteners and first graders in particular) busy in the garden is important, so find parent volunteers to help out. Have a menu of age-appropriate activities. It is important to establish how to "be" in the garden: calm, watchful, focused, attentive, and interested. These behaviors should be modeled and taught from the very first garden class and reinforced throughout the school year. As you move through the year and students get used to coming to the garden, it will become easier to focus their attention for longer periods of time.

Model a positive approach to learning

Many students have never thought about the learning that goes on outside of the classroom. Of course they do it all the time. They are constantly soaking up information around them. Remind students

that when they are doing a free-choice activity, such as looking for bugs, burning ants (they will eventually figure out how to do this with the hand lenses), or picking a bouquet of flowers for the front office, that they are learning. Occasionally ask students after they have had an open garden class (no scheduled lesson or activity) what they learned. It is surprising, and will keep you motivated and inspired about the value of outdoor learning.

Garden time can be full of excitement. The challenge is focusing it.

Be prepared

Like any veteran teacher, you will quickly discover the value of adequately preparing for class. There are some garden activities that you will be able to do on a whim like weeding or watering. Others, such as harvesting or planting, demand a little prep time. And lessons require thoughtful planning. Take the time for these preparations as they will save you panic and headache during class time.

Magnifying lenses have many uses. This is a better use of the sun's energy.

More involved activities require prep time to assemble materials.

Divide and conquer

Most class sizes range between twenty and thirty students. Commanding their collective attention in the garden for a detailed task is a tall order. As we've mentioned, dividing the class is a helpful technique. Parent volunteers can lead half of the students in an activity while you work with the other half on building a trellis, planting a bed of carrots, or assembling seed screens. Or, direct half of the class toward an unsupervised activity such as journaling, watering, weeding, or looking for slugs and snails or other pests. Working with a smaller group of students will allow you to offer more individual attention and the freedom to explore more complex activities in depth. It is useful to address the whole group with the plan for the afternoon, and then to regroup again at the end of the class to reflect.

Appoint student leaders

Appoint a student leader in each garden class. This person might be responsible for getting the clipboards and pencils out of the tool shed, or for setting up part of the cooking station, or for leading a small group activity. During a harvest feast, the student leader might begin a conversation with the class once everyone has sat down together to eat. They might lead a small group to feed the worm bin. And at the end of each class, the student leader is responsible for gathering the pencils and clipboards and returning them to the tool shed. Not only will this be a position that students clamor for, it will also help spread garden ownership (and shorten your prep time!)

Attach lanyards to hand lenses and magnifying glasses

Small things inevitably get lost in the garden. Attach lanyards to tiny hand lenses and magnifying glasses so that students can wear them around their necks while exploring the finer details of the garden. Return them to the shed in their own container with the number of lenses marked on the side. String and shoelaces are not recommended as they invariably get tangled up together and it is time consuming to pass them out.

MAINTENANCE TIPS

The school garden is an outdoor classroom where students learn by doing. Many school garden coordinators and parents make the mistake of burdening themselves with much of the "heavy lifting" when it comes to garden maintenance. We are actually depriving our students of numerous learning opportunities if we do not let them plant, compost, mulch, feed the worms, weed, water, make signs, hunt for pests, and build the trellis. There is pleasure in hard work, and with it comes a sense of ownership. Take the time to show your students how to properly steward a piece of land, care for vegetables, and amend the soil. As an educator you must encourage your students to get their hands dirty, let them make mistakes, and gently correct them as needed. They will take these skills with them beyond school and into life, embedded into their muscle and memory.

Water with rainmakers

Rainmakers are an excellent alternative to an irrigation system. These watering cups are made simply from old yogurt containers or orange juice jugs with their tops cut out. With a hot nail or the sharp point of a knife, punch holes in the bottom of the container through which the water will escape. Place a number of large five-gallon buckets filled with water throughout the garden and distribute the rainmakers among them. Rainmakers offer a number of advantages. Much like rain falling on the earth, the water that showers from the bottom of rainmakers is gentle on the soil, and reduces puddles and the drowning of seeds or seedlings. Eventually rainmakers will breakdown and should be recycled and replaced. However, the main advantages of rainmakers are that they are free and that they do not need to be filled by a hose, which inevitably needs to be monitored by an adult.

In fact, handing a student the garden hose is not recommended. You will probably do it once, but not likely twice. It takes some skill to cover the hose opening with a thumb to evenly and gently spray the water, which young students might not have. Seeds and seedlings get

> **Class management tips:**
>
> ✓ *Model a positive approach to learning.*
>
> ✓ *Be prepared.*
>
> ✓ *Divide the class into smaller groups.*
>
> ✓ *Appoint student leaders in each class.*
>
> ✓ *Attach lanyards to hand lenses and magnifying glasses.*

Summer watering will result in a fall harvest.

Rainmaker in action. *Photo by Stephanie Ma*

drowned; kids fight over control of the hose; and pretty soon everyone is sopping wet. It can be fun, but not necessarily advisable. A rose or spray nozzle that attaches to the end of the hose will solve the manual issue, but not the behavioral one.

We never installed irrigation at the Alice Fong Yu school garden. Instead, we collected used yogurt containers, orange juice jugs, or any other one or two quart plastic vessel and stippled the bottoms with nail sized holes. These containers would be placed throughout the garden, as would five gallon buckets filled with water. The students would submerge the yogurt containers and fill them with water, lift and carry them over the beds in even swaths, the water showering down onto the soil. "Rain-makers" are what we affectionately called these humble tools. Watering was a convenient unsupervised task that I could send half the class to do while I worked with the other half on something more detailed. I constantly had a select set of assignments that I knew I could leave my students to complete without a watchful eye. —RKP

Be courteous to custodial staff

After spending time in the garden, students' shoes and most likely their clothes will be somewhat dirty. Be courteous to your custodial staff by placing a doormat outside the garden for the kids to wipe their feet on as they leave. Be sure to keep an eye out for the space surrounding the garden as well; sweep up errant sand, dirt, or clippings and have students pick up garbage.

Plan for summer maintenance

Summer maintenance of a school garden includes different duties, depending on your school community as well as your climate. In areas with mild winters where you can grow year-round, the summer may be a period where the beds lay fallow. They can be mulched with compost and straw and allowed to rest during the dry summer. In this case, the microorganisms in the soil, would appreciate a bit of summer water. In areas where summer is the primary growing season, a maintenance schedule should be created for watering and weeding to carry the crops and other plants over to the fall when the students return. Or perhaps there is a summer program that utilizes the space. In either climatic circumstance, it is best to begin the school year in the fall with the garden somewhat ready to be planted or harvested or both.

At an end-of-the-year school event have a sign-up sheet ready, divided by the weeks of the summer, and ask parents to take over the garden maintenance for a week or two. Collect their names, contact e-mails, and phone numbers. Send a brief e-mail highlighting the jobs that need to be done over the summer: watering, weeding, and harvesting (if possible). Also include the schedule in this e-mail. In urban areas, the school garden serves as a park of sorts where parents and kids can go during the summer to relax, play, or even grow their own food if space permits. Throughout the summer someone should periodically remind families of their commitment to take care of the garden.

An outdoor sink is an asset to any school garden. A plumber in the parent community can help put it together.

Inventory the parent community for skills and support

Finding skilled adult hands for garden projects is necessary. Inventory your parent (or neighborhood) population for arborists, carpenters, plumbers, and landscapers. Your school garden might need some tree pruning, a new shed, an outdoor sink, or some new plant borders. Inviting parents or interested neighbors to participate in the improvement of the garden space builds ownership and pride in the school.

Occasionally the garden will require the use of a pickup truck for bales of straw, construction materials, loads of soil, mulch, or compost, or flats of seedlings and plants. At the end of the day, when parents are picking their students up from school, make a note of who comes with a pickup. Make a plan to invite that person to a garden committee meeting or simply inquire individually as to whether they would be willing to pick up and deliver needed materials. Or, place a posting on your school's Web site, parent e-mail list, or newsletter looking for parents who might share their truck on occasion. Trucks can also be rented hourly for a workday when no pickup trucks are available from the school community. In urban areas, car-share companies that rent trucks for a few hours are popular with school gardens.

Schedule workdays

Schedule a spring and fall workday where skilled adult hands can help keep your school garden functioning as an outdoor classroom. Projects such as building benches, repairing beds, constructing retaining walls, installing a new whiteboard, or updating an outdoor seating space can be tackled during a workday. Keep a running list of improvements that could be made with a bigger group of people.

Promote workdays in the school newsletter, parent e-mail list, or on an announcement bulletin board within the school. Be sure to tap older students who can fulfill community service hours in the garden during a workday. And remember to feed your volunteers with healthy and hearty snacks as this will keep them happy and willing to show up in the future. Workdays bring people together for a common purpose and result in the overall enhancement of the school.

Look for used tools and equipment

Tools sold half century ago were made to last, constructed with hickory or oak and forged metal. A sharp eye will locate them in a garage or estate sale and they are usually a bargain. While some tools will certainly have to be bought at the local hardware store, ask a parent who enjoys weekend flea markets or garage sales to keep an eye out. Also, encourage your parent community to donate their used or unwanted tools to the school garden.

TIPS ON GENERATING GARDEN SUPPORT

Remain earnest in fostering a spirit of invitation and courtesy within the community in order to maintain the energy surrounding the garden program at your school. Be thoughtful about inviting parents to become involved, attend gatherings or classes in the garden, or help out on workdays. Often parents need to be reached out to individually as they might not respond to a mass e-mail or newsletter. Show them that this project needs their skills and that you would like them to be a part of the garden committee.

Garden program support tips:

» *Present at kindergarten night.*

» *Present at back-to-school night.*

» *Ask for specific donations: create a wish list.*

» *Throw a year-end garden party and recognize volunteers.*

Mullein's soft leaves are great for explorations of the senses.

Present at kindergarten night

Most likely your school will have a night where incoming kindergarten parents will be briefed on the workings of their child's new school. This is an opportunity not be missed for garden committee recruitment. Ask if you can make a short presentation on the garden program, its highlights, and its needs. Come prepared with a way to capture e-mails and phone numbers. Incorporating new blood into the program each year is critical as students move on through the grades and parents inevitably focus their energy in different directions.

Present at back-to-school night

Build the visibility and support for the garden program at back-to-school night each fall. Parents are gearing up for another year and are ripe for new information and looking for ways to get involved. Prepare a presentation board with pictures from garden classes and information on why you *need* them to participate in the program, either on the committee or as a volunteer. Be prepared to collect names and contact information!

Ask for specific donations

Have a garden wish list detailing items the garden needs such as a new wheelbarrow, more hand trowels, a pair of binoculars, or water buckets. Some parents might find getting involved at this level is as much effort as they can put forth, but nevertheless would like to help out. They can donate tools they no longer use and wheelbarrows, spades, rakes, and compost bins may inexplicably appear in your garden. Print the wish list on recycled paper for school events such as back-to-school night or any other celebration bringing the school community together. Post it in the school newsletter or on the Web site.

Year-end garden party and volunteer appreciation

Have a garden party each spring. Invite the entire community: parents, neighbors, students, administration, and teachers. Find a barbeque and a band. Get parents and students to lead fun activities such as sun prints, face painting, or salsa making. Take this time to publicly appreciate your garden volunteers from the school year. Come prepared with a summer watering sign-up sheet and individually thank those families who can help out. The garden is vibrant in the spring, show off how pleasant it is to sit and enjoy this outside space at school.

8.

PLANTING, HARVESTING, AND COOKING IN THE GARDEN

Food-system gardens force us to realize that eating is an agricultural activity. The work that goes into producing food is hidden from us in the grocery store and this prevents us from connecting to what we eat in a deeper way. What fuels our bodies? How much food do we need? Where does our food come from? How much energy is needed to feed a family? How does the land provide? What is the real cost of growing a meal? School gardens illustrate what a food system looks like, from planting to harvest. They teach important lessons about how we nourish ourselves. In this chapter we will discuss techniques for using a school garden to teach about food systems. We will discuss ways to negotiate planting, harvesting, and cooking with students; what crops are handy in this setting; and what tools are useful during this process. These gardening tasks require care, but with strategic planning and preparation students are adept at taking them on. Certain crops are must haves in the school garden as they are easy to grow, easy to clean, and easy to prepare. Along with a primer on these must-have edibles, we will also provide several tried and true recipes that have been tested and approved by many students over the years in the back of the book.

EASY SCHOOL GARDEN CROPS

Cole crops	Snowy winter planting times	Rainy winter planting times
Broccoli	June–August	February–September
Brussels sprouts	June–August	April–June
Cauliflower	June–August	March–April, September–October
Collards	June–August	January–February, July–September
Kale	June–August	January–February, July–September
Greens	Snowy winter planting times	Rainy winter planting times
Arugula (rocket)	April–August	Year round
Chard	April	Year round
Lettuce	April–June, July	Year round
Mustard	April–June	January–March, July–September
Spinach	April–June	January–March, September–December
Root crops	Snowy winter planting times	Rainy winter planting times
Beets	April–June	February, September
Carrots	May–June	April, August–September
Radishes	April–September	Year round
Tubers	Snowy winter planting times	Rainy winter planting times
Potatoes	April–June	March
Sunchokes	April–May	Year round
Alliums	Snowy winter planting times	Rainy winter planting times
Bunching onions	April–May	July–September
Garlic	March–April	October–November
Leeks	April–May	Year round
Legumes	Snowy winter planting times	Rainy winter planting times
Beans	May–June	April–July
Peas	May–June	Year round
Sun-loving fruits	Snowy winter planting times	Rainy winter planting times
Cucumber	May–June	April–June
Peppers	May–June	May–June

Sun-loving fruits (cont.)	Snowy winter planting times	Rainy winter planting times
Squash (many varieties)	May–June	March, June
Tomato	May–June	May–June

Edible flowers	Snowy winter planting times	Rainy winter planting times
Borage	May–June	Year round
Calendula	May–June	January–June
Nasturtium	May–June	January–May
Sunflower	May–June	February–August

Perennial herbs	Snowy winter planting times	Rainy winter planting times
Rosemary	May–June	Year round
Thyme	May–June	Year round
Sage	May–June	Year round
Mint	May–June	Year round
Chives	May–June	Year round
Oregano	May–June	Year round

Annual herbs	Snowy winter planting times	Rainy winter planting times
Parsley	April, August	Spring, fall
Coriander (cilantro)	June	January
Dill	April–June	April–June
Basil	June	May–July

PLANTING

Planting vegetables from seed or from small seedlings is a delicate task. While it may be daunting to do this with an excited class of second graders, a little breakage here and a little seed drowning there will not matter much. Students love this part of gardening. Planting is a necessary experience for student and while it *does* require a bit of care, they will learn to plant properly with good instruction and demonstration. Often it is a student's first experience tending a garden, so be prepared and plant a little extra. Excess can be given away to a food bank or sold at a school event.

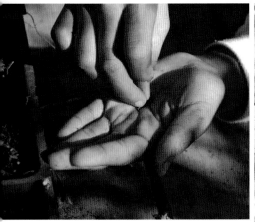

Students planting mustard seeds.

Healthy seedlings, ready to be planted out.

Two effective planting methods are direct seeding or planting with seedlings. Most crops can be directly seeded in a school garden, but you may bring your garden a few weeks closer to harvest by planting out seedlings purchased at a local nursery. A good nursery will carry a wide variety of vegetable seedlings for you to choose from. Established garden projects sometimes decide to invest in a greenhouse and produce their own seedlings.

A note on class management when planting

Both direct seeding as well as planting seedlings require similar student management. Divide your class into smaller groups when planting. Have one or two tasks or activities on hand that the other students

Student management during planting:

✓ *Divide the class into smaller groups and rotate them.*

✓ *Have a menu of activities for the remaining students.*

✓ *Encourage parent volunteer help on planting day.*

✓ *Discuss crop details at planting site with smaller group.*

✓ *Broadcast tiny seeds.*

✓ *Individually plant larger seeds.*

Harvesting broccoli. *Photo by Linda Myers*

can easily do while one group is planting with you and requiring all your attention. If you have parent volunteers they can lead one of these tasks. It is easier to explain the planting process and demonstrate the care it requires to a smaller group of six to ten students. Plan to discuss the crop you are working with at the planting site: the seed size in relation to seed depth; the time until germination and harvest (if direct seeding); or the number of days until maturity (if planting seedlings). The back of a typical seed packet has specific information; have your students find and share it with the group if their age and literacy level allows. Take advantage of the smaller audience and ask questions that encourage deeper thinking: "Why do we need to space the chard plants like this?" or "What is happening to the seed before it germinates?"

Direct seeding

Direct seeding means planting seeds outside in the garden soil without first starting them in a greenhouse. Planting a seed directly in the ground begins a life cycle that students will continue to observe throughout the school year from germination to flower to seed again. Broadcast seeding is useful for manipulating tiny seeds (carrots, radishes, beets, lettuce, and spinach). Larger seeds such as squash, peas, and beans can be individually planted by students. Soil temperature is an important factor in seed germination. Pay attention to when you plant during the year, the climate, and the weather conditions as these factors will affect germination rates. Seed packets usually mention the

SEED SAVING

In a school garden some crops and flowers should be left to go to seed. Students should understand that pulling a carrot out of the ground interrupts the life cycle of that plant. However, if students are encouraged to leave a few carrots undisturbed they will see the plant shift from root growth into seed production. Another teaching opportunity will arise later in the collection of seeds from the flowers. Seed saving is a powerful activity for students in the garden; it is a life skill.

Easy seed saving plants: calendula, coriander, godetia, sunflower, beets, chard, nigella

Seed saving at a glance:

» Threshing and winnowing: separating seed from husk and then from chaff

» Storage: properly preserving seeds to prevent spoilage

» Germination testing: forcing seeds to germinate to test viability

» Record keeping: what was planted; when and where the seed was collected

See chapter 9, "Year-Round Garden Lessons and Activities," and Resources for seed-saving activities and seed suppliers.

Seed screens are easily made.

ideal soil temperature for a particular seed. Don't forget that tiny seeds need constant moisture; they won't survive a long dry spell.

Broadcast seeding means randomly sowing seeds over a prescribed area by throwing them; and it is a useful method for tiny, hard to manipulate seeds. It can also be a good method for small radish, beet, and spinach seeds. Let students help you prepare the bed. Have them rake the area clean of large debris and pull back a thin layer of soil to expose the planting surface. Hand out a pinch of seeds to each student as they encircle the area. Demonstrate how to evenly distribute the seeds over the surface, then have the students do the same. Distribute the soil on the margins of the bed in the same fashion to cover the seeds. End by lightly tamping the soil with everyone's hands before watering. Broadcast seeding provides an alternative to traditional rows of carrots or lettuces, and is a great time saver when working with younger students.

If you do want to plant carrots or lettuce in rows, place the tiny seeds in a small bowl and add a little bit of fine horticultural sand and mix. This is a good way to provide a little "weight" to the seeds and it also distributes the seeds nicely as the students place this mixture in rows along small trenches.

Germinated seeds that have been broadcast will require some thinning. Students are capable of doing this and I admire their small clever fingers when they do this task. Reference the seed packet for spacing requirements and demonstrate how to carefully reduce the number of

Students planting lettuce seeds.

Photo by Diana Samuelson

- -

Sturdy trellises can be lashed together by students using twine and branches.

sprouts. Some crops *can* remain somewhat bunched however—lettuce lends itself well to a method called "cut and come again." The first round of leafy greens can be cut, preserving the crown, and a second growth of leaves will provide a harvest a few weeks later.

Large seeds are easy to plant with students of any age. One or two fingers are all you need to dig a small hole to the appropriate depth and plant large seeds. (Planting depth should be approximately one and a half to two times the width of the seed.) Peas, beans, and cucurbits such as squash or gourds all have large seeds. Demonstrate where to plant, appropriate spacing, and how to mound the soil if needed. Peas or beans that climb require a trellis. Have students make one out of bamboo poles or even discarded tree branches.

Each year brought a different style of trellis to the garden. After pruning the massive pines on the school grounds, we lashed the leftover bendable branches together to create funky looking archways over the beds. We weaved twine in between the branches for snap peas to climb. Another year we were more organized and parent volunteers helped drive tree stakes into a few of the beds. Chicken wire was then spread across the gap and nailed to the stakes. These trellises were very sturdy and lasted several years with sweet peas and sugar snap peas constantly adorning them. —RKP

Seedlings

Many crops are more convenient to plant as seedlings as it saves time. Developing a relationship with your local nursery can have its benefits. Often nurseries will offer discounts to school programs and you can obtain young plants at a reduced cost. Cole crops (cabbage family, which includes broccoli), chard, tomatoes, and peppers mature faster in the garden if planted as seedlings. This is also true of alliums such as onions, leeks, garlic, and chives. Look for robust green leaves on stout plants when selecting seedlings from the nursery. Nursery plants that have been sitting too long often look stressed: too tall for their small containers, root hairs protruding from the bottom of the pot, and yellow leaves at their base.

Teach students how to correctly remove a young plant from its pot by massaging the base and gently pushing from the bottom of the pot while not pulling the stem. Take note of the roots; if they are tightly bound show the students how to gently untangle them. This prepares the plant for new growth and prevents it from becoming root bound. Dig a hole that reflects the size of the seedling's root mass. Place the seedling in the hole and gently pull the soil over the area and press down firmly. Explain that tamping around the base of the plant eliminates any air pockets that could dry out the roots. Have the students plant the other seedlings in the same fashion. Check each planting with the students to ensure it has been sufficiently tamped down and is as upright as can be, and have them give the seedling a generous drink of water before moving on.

DIRECT SEED VERSUS SEEDLINGS

Direct seed	Seedlings
Arugula (rocket)	Broccoli
Beans	Brussels sprouts
Beets	Cauliflower
Carrots	Chard
Cucumber (or seedlings)	Collards
Lettuce	Garlic (cloves)
Mustard	Leeks
Peas	Onions
Radishes	Peppers
Spinach	Potatoes (tubers)
Squash	Sunchokes (tubers)
Turnips	Tomato

Planting potatoes and sunchokes

Kids listen with wide eyes when you explain how potatoes grow. They are easy to plant and grow to become buried treasure for students. They also illustrate another fascinating plant reproductive scheme. Botanically, potatoes are underground stems and their "eyes" are buds from where the new plant will grow. In school gardens, potatoes are most often grown from seed potatoes, which are small walnut-sized tubers that will produce a new plant. Once the potato is buried the buds grow to the surface in search of the sun. The new leaves then photosynthesize and send the energy to be stored underground as more potatoes. Purchase a bag of certified disease-free seed potatoes and have the students bury them in trenches in a bed. Space them at least ten to twelve inches apart and at least four inches below the surface of the soil. Mound the soil around your plant to keep new tubers covered as they only form on the stem above the original seed

Healthy seedlings adapt quickly to their new home.

139

potato. New potatoes turn green if they are exposed to the sun for a period of time and this green area produces a toxin that can be harmful to ingest.

Sunchokes (or Jerusalem artichokes) are also grown from tubers. This sunflower species is noted for its edible tuber that can be peeled and eaten raw or boiled and pureed into a hearty soup. The flavor of sunchokes resembles artichoke hearts, and they are legendary for their rather "windy" effects. Tubers can be ordered from seed catalogs, but are often shared among gardeners. They are buried in the ground, approximately two or three inches deep and one foot apart. Sunchokes grow into tall cheerful stalks with sunflowers. They bloom throughout the summer and are harvested in the fall.

NURTURING THE CROP

Once the crops are in the ground, the process of caring for and protecting them begins. Generally, remember that caring for crops requires routine tasks, all of which should be done by the students. Regular watering, weeding, mulching, thinning, and being vigilant about other critters enjoying and destroying your plants are activities that students enjoy.

HARVEST

The thrill of harvesting in the garden generates a lot of excitement; students gather the bounty, amazed by what sun and soil can produce. Without good preparation, though, the chaos and excitement can overwhelm the process. Teaching harvesting rituals, careful hygiene, and a proper order of events on harvest day will help you in the long run. For instance, students should know that after you have finished your introduction, they are to go to the bucket of soapy water to wash their hands. They know to get the container of scissors from the shed and place it on the cooking table, and they will be able to find the cutting boards, salad spinner, and plates and forks for their fellow students. Students feel independent and empowered when they can negotiate the garden systems on their own. Teaching rituals of proper food preparation and standardized harvesting methods will ensure a fun, meaningful harvest party.

Different crops have different harvesting requirements. Greens can be cut or pinched. Root crops and others that grow underground require some excavation and scrubbing. Students know they are free to pick and eat "at will" sugar-snap peas, snow peas, strawberries, beans, cherry tomatoes, and edible flowers such as borage and spicy nasturtium. The crops mentioned in this section are hardy and require relatively little fuss. They are also crops that every school garden can experience at different times in the school year no matter what the local climate is.

EDIBLE CROPS BY HARVESTING METHOD

Cut	Dig	Pick at will
Lettuce	Potatoes	Peas
Spinach	Sunchokes	Beans
Chard	Beets	Carrots
Collards	Carrots	Edible flowers
Mustard	Garlic	Cherry tomatoes
Bunching onions	Onions	Berries
Chives	Leeks	
Herbs	Radishes	
Bok choi		
Arugula (rocket)		

Greens

As the parts of the plant that conduct photosynthesis, edible greens grow fast and copiously compared to the fruit, which takes time to ripen the seeds within. All dark, leafy greens (kale, chard, collards, lettuce, spinach) are packed with nutrients and are astoundingly easy to harvest. Students can snip leaves from the plants with a pair of child-sized scissors or gently tear them off. Some students prefer using scissors for harvesting greens and this ensures that a whole plant isn't pulled out by accident. As is mentioned earlier, lettuce can be planted thickly as a "cut and come again" crop, allowing for multiple harvests.

On harvest day, give each student a specific number of leaves to cut. This gives you control over how much of your crop is being used and how much you will have left for other classes. Depending on class size and the meal, you will vary the number of leaves per student. Usually ten leaves per student will make a generous salad. We have noticed that kindergartners tend to eat very little, whereas older students devour what they are served.

"Salad partyyy!" the class of third graders screamed when I appeared out of the garden shed wearing the orange apron that I always wore on harvest days. I carried two large bowls in my arms and descended the slight slope to the circle of straw bales where the students were waiting.

"What is salad?" I asked, "What crop?" Several hands shot up. I called on them all to reveal the answer in unison: "Lettuce!" they cheered.

A few weeks before, just after the school year started, this same group of third graders prepared one of our raised beds for planting. They added compost, evened out the surface, and drew back a thin layer of the rich, loamy earth to expose the planting area. We broadcast seeded many varieties of lettuce: black-seeded Simpson, Romaine, butter lettuce, red oak leaf, and other heirloom varieties.

Within a week we would begin to anticipate germination—the emergence of hundreds of tiny green mouse ear-like leaves; and now a few weeks later, it was time to celebrate with a salad party. The students each wielded a pair of scissors, ready to harvest.

"Each of you will harvest ten leaves of lettuce, and you know where to cut, right?" I asked. They did. They learned that if you cut the leaves above the crown this same plant would then continue to sprout new, young leaves for yet another harvest a few weeks later—a "cut and come again" crop. And that meant more salad parties.—RKP

(far left) A salad party.

(center) Cut and come again. *Photo by Brooke Hieserich*

(near left) Students with newly dug potatoes. *Photo by Jean Moshofsky-Butler*

Root crops and potatoes

Harvesting root crops such as radishes and carrots is as fun as finding buried treasure. Students can pull them directly out of the ground and there is certain to be discussion about who harvested the biggest root. Tools can be useful when excavating a bed of potatoes, or prying a reluctant carrot out of the soil; have trowels or a digging fork ready. Digging for potatoes, in particular, is one of the best gardening activities for any age group. Locating the firm rounds within the loamy soil is like finding gold. The transformation that takes place between the simple task of putting the potato in the ground and digging out the next generation of fresh new potatoes is miraculous.

Potatoes can be dug once the flowers or leaves of the plant have faded. Not much explanation is required for harvest; simply demonstrate how to carefully find the new potatoes without damaging them. (It is easy to accidentally slice them in half with a trowel.) Place a bucket of trowels next to the bed and have a bowl nearby to put the potatoes in once they have been unearthed. Scrub and rinse them in two buckets of clean, cold water.

The same harvesting method, using trowels if necessary, can be applied to sunchokes, the tubers of which remain buried in the soil after the leaves and flowers fade in the fall. Carrots, radishes, onions, leeks, and turnips will all also require some scrubbing after being pulled or pried from the earth.

Radishes, I thought, were the perfect crop for kindergarteners; they are easy to plant and they sprout extremely fast. The first year I taught in the garden I planted them with every class, it seemed. When the kindergartners harvested their first radish crop they held with pride the tight little red spheres that looked like candy. They washed and eagerly bit into their radishes. Immediately they loved them; I was so excited. Then a moment later the smiles turned to frowns and tongues started franticly pushing radish slaw out of their mouths and onto the ground. Too bitter, too spicy! All around the garden were little spits of radish. We cut back on our production from then on. —RKP

"At will" crops

You'll be hard pressed to find a single sugar snap pea on the vine in a school garden. Certain crops should be planted copiously for students to pick and nibble on at will. Strawberries, beans, snow peas, cherry tomatoes, and edible flowers such as borage and nasturtium are all fair game in the garden. Teach students to harvest carefully with two hands; one holding the vine or branch stable, the other pulling gently at the fruit.

Harvesting is the culmination of months of work in the garden, and is only surpassed by preparing and eating the harvest.

THE FEAST

Eating from the garden is a powerful and memorable activity in the outdoor classroom. It directly engages the senses of sight, smell, taste, and touch. After a day of sitting at a desk, coming to the garden allows for very different kinds of learning. As mentioned, studies have shown that students exposed to fruits and vegetables through a school garden are much more likely to incorporate them into their eating habits later in life. Countless parents have reported that their once salad-hating child was now eating greens at home and was even schooling them on how to properly make vinaigrette dressing. Growing, caring for, and harvesting food give students a new perspective on vegetables and eating.

A note on proper hygiene and zero waste

Proper hygiene while eating from the garden is important. We recommend conducting some research into your local health codes. Meanwhile, for preparing and eating snacks in the garden, there are a few techniques for ensuring cleanliness. Before handling food always have a warm bucket of soapy water available for the students to wash their hands.

On harvest day, set out two separate buckets of clean water to wash greens and other vegetables. One bucket should be used for an initial scrub. Rinse everything again for good measure in the second bucket. A variety of brushes are useful for stubborn dirt. Occasionally, scrub these buckets down with a little soap and rinse well.

Wash any dishes, utensils, and cooking equipment such as pots and pans in a hot dishwasher after use. Otherwise have a dish-washing station set up for the end of class: one bin of warm soapy water, one for a rinse, and a last one with diluted bleach water to kill any pathogens. Please note that these are general guidelines and that you should research and develop appropriate hygiene standards for your particular school garden. Most outdoor picnics end with garbage cans overflowing with paper plates, plastic forks and knives, plastic cups, and napkins. School garden feasts are similar to a picnic but, instead of filling landfills with the debris of this style of event, school garden feasts are a ripe opportunity to instill a zero waste ethic.

Create a waste system in your garden that teaches students about where their "trash" ends up. One bin should be marked "compost" for all food scraps and other easily biodegradable items. The second should be marked "recyclables" for items such as plastic water bottles, cans, foil, and glass. The third should be marked "landfill" for items for which you have no alternative such as plastic wrap. For clarity, the bins might be different colors (green, blue, and black). Teach students how to properly dispose of items from their lunch or a garden snack. You'll be surprised at how little goes into the landfill bin when you are able to divert trash to either compost or recycling. Create a competition on how little each class sends to the landfill.

Compost any paper plates. If compost systems do not exist yet, invest in reusable plates and forks. Wash dishes, as described above, if a dishwasher is not available at your school. Buy supplies such as oil and vinegar in bulk and recycle empty bottles. Send nothing to the landfill if at all possible.

Set up

A large plastic container with a tight fitting lid in your garden shed labeled "Cooking" will be one of your best organizational tools. The container will have supplies such as paper or reusable plates, reusable forks, cutting boards, knives, a salad spinner, a wok, a small bucket, a portable stove, a few large bowls, tongs, a jar for making dressings in, a mortar and pestle for crushing garlic or nuts, and biodegradable/non-toxic dish soap. In an additional "Condiments" container, keep nonperishable supplies such as soy sauce or tamari, salt and pepper, vinegar, and spices of any sort. Keep perishables like Dijon mustard, olive oil, and lemons in the school refrigerator.

A broad, sturdy table that students can gather around is an ideal staging area. Parent volunteers are very useful on feast days to help set up, cut, clean up, etc. Place the appropriate supplies on the table: stove for heating if needed, bowls for harvested and washed vegetables, salad spinner if appropriate, tongs, cutting boards and knives, plates and forks, and any other necessary ingredients.

COOKING

Some crops can be eaten right off the vine, some can be prepared and eaten raw (salads), while others require cooking (sautés). We offer a few examples of how to prepare a harvest from the school garden. Don't be afraid to experiment.

Off the vine; out of the ground

Carrots, strawberries, beans, snap and snow peas, cherry tomatoes, and edible flowers provide immediate snacks in the garden. Wash and eat! The connection between student and food created in that tasting is direct and indelible.

Salads

Salads of mixed lettuces as well as chopped salads of broccoli and carrots are the easiest meals to prepare with students; they require no heat. Whip up a vinaigrette dressing with olive oil, vinegar, herbs, salt and pepper, Dijon, and maybe some shallots or garlic from the garden. Students can help measure ingredients, harvest and chop herbs, and shake the dressing in a spare jar. Add this to your greens or chopped broccoli salad and you're ready to eat.

Salad parties created with the many varieties of lettuce deserve special note. They are easy to grow and prepare, and they are a great initiation to a lifetime affinity for vegetables and healthy eating habits. Fresh, crisp lettuce mixed in a bowl with calendula and nasturtium, herbs, and tasty vinaigrette makes for a quick and yummy snack.

Cooking over a stove in the garden

A quick stir-fry of onions, chard, and soy sauce is delicious added to cellophane rice noodles that have been soaking in warm water. A sauté of chard, collard greens, and pea shoots is accented nicely by a little honey and lemon. A great way to bulk up a meager harvest is to prepare pasta beforehand and add it to your sauté of greens. These meals can be thrown together in the wok and served immediately. A single-burner butane stove or a cast iron camp stove that connects to a propane tank works extremely well. Search online for either of these products. They typically cost between $60 and $90.

A sun oven (also called a solar oven) is another great piece of equipment to have in the garden—use it a to roast potatoes or bake cookies. There are designs to build your own available on the Internet, or you

Quick steps to prepare for a cooking day:

✓ *Identify parent volunteers.*

✓ *Check for adequate supplies such as plates and perishables.*

✓ *Set up hand-washing station.*

✓ *Set up dish-washing station.*

✓ *Set up produce-washing buckets.*

✓ *Set up stove and cooking area.*

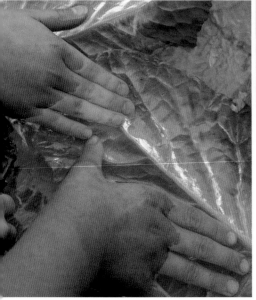

Washing collards.

- -

Using a stove in the garden.

can purchase one. Although they can be costly (prices range from $100 to $250), they are well worth the expense.

Put potatoes in the oven in the morning and allow them to cook most of the day until the class arrives in the afternoon. (Be sure that the oven reflectors follow the sun as the day goes on or the temperature will drop significantly.)

Once food has been prepared, have students serve each other. On the serving table you should have tongs, a pile of plates and forks, and perhaps a couple of sliced baguettes from a local bakery to supplement. Create a place for students to sit with one another and enjoy the meal or snack. Sit with them. Encourage discussion. Listen to reactions and comments. This is one of the calmer moments in the garden with students. Creating this environment during a meal reinforces the good habits of taking the time to eat, sit, and enjoy each other's company.

Planting and harvesting the crops to produce the feast are daunting steps to accomplish before taking the first bite. Strategic planning and preparation, good clear instruction, and trust in your students can make all of this remarkably easy and fun. Have your systems set up, teach your students rituals, and stick to them. At the end of the day, your students will go home practitioners of organic gardening, ambassadors of healthy eating, and champions of fresh, local food.

9.

YEAR-ROUND GARDEN LESSONS AND ACTIVITIES

The garden is a rich environment for learning. Garden coordinators often create their own lessons out of sheer ingenuity and inspiration from the natural phenomena that are revealed in the schoolyard. You may find that you enjoy creating your own curriculum as well, or you may want to reach out to established gardens for their tried and true lessons and activities and perhaps even borrow their purchased curriculum to get started. Garden-based curricula are numerous and wide ranging; a list of curriculum resources is provided in the back of this book.

Throughout this chapter, we have provided some sample lesson plans and garden activities, arranged by season to make it easier to apply them in the various regions and climate zones where school gardens exist and to give you a sense of what is possible in a school garden throughout the year. Lessons have been adapted from existing garden-based curriculum, and activities are short, seasonal tasks and learning games to engage students in the garden. Remember to have fun with the students in the garden, make room for nature's improvisation, and emphasize to the teachers the importance of this hands-on, full-sensory experience.

SEASONAL SCHOOL GARDEN LESSONS AND ACTIVITIES

Here are sample lessons for fall, winter, spring, and the entire school year. We have also suggested seasonal tasks and activities to give you an idea of a year in a school garden.

FALL

Seed Saving: Preserving the Legacy 151
Look Lively.................................... 153
Stem, Root, Leaf, or Fruit?...................... 154

WINTER

Zip Code Seeds 157
Habitat Riddles 158
An Introduction to Worm Composting 160

SPRING

Land Scarcity 163
Graphing Plant Growth 163
Interviewing Local Farmers 165

ENTIRE SCHOOL YEAR

Garden Scavenger Hunt........................ 166
Pollution Soup 167

The outdoor classroom.

SEED SAVING: PRESERVING THE LEGACY

Adapted from Jessica Bean, Heather Russell, Kae Bosman-Clark, and others, "Seed Saving: Preserving the Legacy, Planning for Next Year." in the Earth Steward Gardener Curriculum. Copyright © 2007 Cultivating Community, Portland, Maine

Objective

To teach the concept of seed saving by collecting tomato seeds from this year's garden for planting the next season.

Materials

✓ 3 or 4 heirloom tomatoes

✓ Cutting board

✓ Knife

✓ 3 mason jars (one-quart size)

✓ Cheesecloth

✓ 3 rubber bands

✓ Small jar or other container for storing seeds

Key concepts

» The fruit of the tomato we grew this year holds the seeds that we need for next year. Because we have successfully cared for this plant, it has produced seed-holding fruit. We can reap the benefits and grow these fruits again next year.

» We want to save seeds from plants that we liked the best: the biggest, tastiest, and fastest growing. The seeds from these plants are most likely to resemble their parents and grow into plants that we like next year.

» All of our food crops were once wild plants. By selecting seeds and saving them to plant again next year, we are participating in an ancient relationship with our food crops. We get to experience the interdependence of agriculture; they need us to grow, and we need them to nourish ourselves.

Note

This activity must be done with open-pollinated, heirloom variety plants. Hybrids, which many of our crop varieties are today, will not produce offspring as predictably as their parents. Seed saving can be done with all food crops, but we recommend starting with tomatoes because they do not cross-pollinate and you don't need to do any fancy planning. For further reading on seed saving or to learn the specifics for other crops, check out Suzanne Ashworth's book *Seed to Seed* (Seed Savers Exchange 2002). Open-pollinated heirloom varieties of tomatoes and other crops are available through Fedco seeds (www.fedcoseeds.org), Johnny's Selected Seeds (www.johnnyseeds.com), or from the Seed Savers Exchange (www.seedsavers.org).Or go to your local farmer's market in the late summer and fall and you will find heirloom tomatoes that you can save the seeds from.

Activity

The first step is to go out into the garden and find a tomato plant that you want to save seeds from. Look for the strongest, fastest growing plants with the tastiest fruit. Decide together on the traits that are most important to you, and choose fruit from the plant that best embodies them. This is a good basic genetics lesson for kids. Children take after their parents in many ways; and the same is true of tomatoes. So, by choosing the plant we think is best, we will expect to find those same traits that we admire in its offspring.

Next, bring the tomatoes in, wash them off, and put them on the cutting board. Discuss the process of germination with your students. Some questions you might ask them are:

» What does a seed need to sprout? (Answer: They need moisture and warmth.)

» What do you think it is like in the middle of a tomato? (Answer: It's probably moist and warm.)

» So why don't tomato seeds start to grow inside the tomato? (And probably no one knows the answer to this one.)

Tomatoes have a protective covering over their seeds, a natural inhibitor to germination. This inhibitor can't be washed off, and until it is removed the tomato seeds won't germinate. The inhibitor can only be eaten away by the bacteria produced as the tomato rots.

The next step is to cut open the tomatoes and squeeze the juice and seeds out evenly into quart mason jars. Label the jars, then fill them about 2/3 full with water, cover them with cheesecloth, and secure it with a rubber band. Place the jars in a warm place and leave them for three days to a week to allow fermentation to take place. As mold grows on the rotting tomatoes, the inhibitor covering the seeds will be eaten off and the viable seeds will sink to the bottom of the jar.

Once it looks like a nice little collection of clean seeds has accumulated on the bottom of the jar, pour the mold off the top and add some more water to let the seeds settle toward the bottom; repeat this process a couple of times until just the clean seeds remain on the bottom. Pour these seeds into a sieve, then dump them on newspaper and spread them out in a sunny spot to dry. Once they are totally dry, put them in a small jar, label it, and store in a cool, dark place until planting time.

Follow-up activities

» Tomatoes were domesticated in warm, tropical areas such as Latin America. When ripened, they fell to the ground and rotted. From the rotting fruits, new fruits grew. How do you think that these plants were domesticated by hunter-gatherer peoples? Would they have noticed this cycle? Understanding the life cycle and ancestry of plants is necessary when you are trying to save their seeds. Plan a creative writing exercise where students describe how they would imagine the lives of the first tomato seed savers. Or have students do research projects on particular plants, where they come from, and how they might have been domesticated.

» There are many science-based investigations that could flow from this activity: genetics, plant origins, plant life cycle, or chemical responses in the process of fermentation. Social studies that could relate to this activity include ancient civilizations and the origins of agriculture.

» "From Generation to Generation: An Activity Guidebook in the Living Tradition of Seed Saving" by Eli Kaufman and produced by Fedco Seeds, is a free curriculum guide full of activities for both elementary and secondary grade levels. It is available for download at http://www.growseed.org/GenerationtoGenernation.pdf

» This activity lends itself well to discussing the importance of preserving diversity in food crops. Two hundred years ago nearly everyone was a seed saver and grew much of their own food. Now it is a dying art. In the last century alone, we have lost more than 75 percent of our crop diversity! Discuss the implications of this diversity loss with your students and why it is important to preserve heirloom varieties and crop diversity.

LOOK LIVELY

Adapted from Life Lab Science Program (Grade 4, "Habitats"), Santa Cruz, California; www.lifelab.org

Introduction

What do you need for survival? How do you meet your survival needs? Could you live anywhere? How about plants and animals? What do the plants in our garden or schoolyard need for survival? What do the animals need? How does our garden help them survive? What if we cleared out all the plants in the garden? What would happen to all the animals?

Objectives

To help students understand what humans, plants, and other animals need for survival and record their ideas.

Materials

✓ Journals

✓ Pencils

✓ Clipboards

A red admiral butterfly is a common school garden visitor.

Activity

» Pair up students and designate one as the "Plant Investigator" and the other one as the "Animal Investigator."

» Take students to the garden and ask each pair to find an observation spot. Ask the pairs to look for an animal on a plant and record in their journals how the animal is using the plant (or the plant is using the animal!). If students cannot find a plant and animal together, tell them to select one plant and one animal in their spot.

» The Animal Investigator observes the animal and records everything it does for five to ten minutes. Encourage students to be specific: if a bee is visiting flowers, investigators should identify or sketch each one; if a caterpillar is eating a leaf, investigators should determine how much of the leaf is consumed during the time period. Suggest that the Animal Investigator draw a map of where the animal goes and what it does.

» The Plant Investigator's job is to sketch and describe the plant within its habitat. Encourage the Plant Investigator to record habitat conditions such as light, moisture, and soil type in order to learn what kind of habitat this plant needs for survival.

STEM, ROOT, LEAF, OR FRUIT?

Adapted from Roberta Jaffe and Gary Appel, *The Growing Classroom* (Addison-Wesley 2001). Developed by Life Lab Science & The National Gardening Association

Description

Students classify foods and spices they eat according to plant parts, and harvest snacks from the garden.

Objectives

To identify and classify the parts of plants we eat.

Materials

✓ Journals

✓ Samples of fresh herbs and spices, from the garden if available, such as: pepper, dill, caraway, cinnamon

✓ Vegetable samples, from the garden if available, such as: carrots, celery, spinach, broccoli, peas, sunflower seeds. Refer to the chart on food categories that follows to choose examples of different categories.

✓ Dips for vegetables, such as cottage cheese, onion dip, or hummous

✓ Cutting boards and knives

Activity

Name some plants that you eat. (List responses on the chalkboard.) Do you eat the whole plant or part of it? Let's list the different parts of plants: root, stem, leaf, bark, flower, fruit, seed. Do you think we eat all of these different parts? (Record predictions.) Can you name the different parts of the plants we listed that you eat? (List the part name(s) next to each plant.)

1. Group students in pairs.

2. Have students make seven category headings in their journals: root, stem, leaf, bark, flower, fruit, seed.

3. Tell them to write each food in one of the categories, according to what part of the plant it is that we eat. For example, a walnut is a seed, and eggplant is a fruit, and so on.

4. To introduce students to the wonderful world of spices, have them use their senses to explore the samples you have collected.

5. Challenge students to try classifying the spices. This tends to be a little more difficult for students, so if they cannot put the spices in the categories, guide them through.

6. Now have the students enjoy their new knowledge. Have them cut up vegetables and use the spices to prepare a dip. Or harvest carrots or peas from the garden and eat.

Questions for discussion

» What is your favorite vegetable?

» Which part of the plant do you eat?

» What is your favorite root, leaf, stem, bark, flower, fruit, or seed?

Follow-up activities

1. Have students describe their last meal in terms of plant parts. For example, a peanut butter and jelly sandwich would be seeds (peanut butter) and crushed fruit (jelly/jam) on ground-up and baked seeds (bread).

2. Have students design a three-course meal composed only of one category. How would they enjoy such a meal?

3. Have students plant a garden bed according to the plant parts they eat, with a section for each category.

FOOD CATEGORIES

Root	Stem	Leaf	Bark	Flower	Fruit	Seed
Carrot	Celery	Basil	Cinnamon	Broccoli	Tomato	Almond
Beet	Kohlrabi	Parsley		Cauliflower	Eggplant	Dill
Radish	Asparagus	Spinach		Nasturtium	Apple	Caraway
Ginger		Lettuce			Banana	Chocolate
		Mint				Bean
						Rice
						Wheat

Zucchini flower.

HOOP HOUSE USE FOR EXTENDING THE SEASONS

In his book *The Winter Harvest Handbook*, Maine farmer Eliot Coleman outlines techniques and methods he uses for growing select crops throughout the snowy winter months. Coleman's farm lies within climatic Zone 5 where the average annual low is between −10 degrees F and −20 degrees F. He found that if he covered certain crops with two layers of protection, first a floating fabric row cover, and then an overarching hoop house (a greenhouse that Coleman prefers to call a "cold house"), he effectively moved that planting area three zones south to Zone 8, where the average annual low is between 10 and 20 degrees F.

During the day, the heat from the sun (which is shining for an efficient amount of time at that latitude during the winter) warms the house enough to keep the temperature above freezing, and crops will survive. Winter crops are adapted to colder temperatures and these layers allow them to persist within their range. Such crops include spinach, chard, certain types of lettuce, Asian greens such as mizuna and tatsoi, and radishes. Growing these crops also depends on a well-timed planting schedule and thorough preparation in the fall.

Coleman's farm is growing crops for market, and he has gone into great depth in explaining how these methods, and others, can be used to make farming economically viable during the coldest months. In a school garden, these techniques could simply be a fascinating way to experiment with your growing season as a part of your garden curriculum for older students. Perhaps you plant a bed of cold-hardy greens and stake a bit of row cover fabric over it to protect it from early frost. You could then follow that by erecting an inexpensive plastic covered hoop house (framed with plastic pipes or wood) to keep the snow off and to trap heat during the day. Students could take measurements of temperature, record growth rates by observing change over time, and record hypotheses for success or failure of crops. There are, no doubt, school gardens that are already extending their growing season in some fashion by using greenhouses; this inexpensive double layer approach might be an interesting way to take the garden one step further, and in colder climates, to enjoy harvests later in the school year.

Further information on climate, day length, garden design, and the history and research related to growing in cold temperatures can be found in *The Winter Harvest Handbook*, which also has lists of supplies and suppliers.

ZIP CODE SEEDS

Adapted from Roberta Jaffe and Gary Appel, *The Growing Classroom* (Addison-Wesley 2001). Developed by Life Lab Science *&* The National Gardening Association

Description

Students will choose a variety of seeds to order from catalogs based upon climate, food crop, and aesthetic preferences.

Objectives

To learn and apply knowledge of climate, plant varieties, consumer preferences, along with the ability to estimate quantities in compiling seed orders.

Materials

✓ A variety of seed catalogs

✓ List of recommended vegetables and flowers to grow in your climate zone. (These can be obtained from your local county agricultural extension, or you can make your own by compiling your annual rainfall, average temperatures, type of soil, number of frost-free days, and amount of direct sun exposure with the needs recommended on seed catalogs or packets.)

✓ Order and obtain catalogs at least six weeks in advance. (Once you are on a mailing list, you will usually receive a catalog every year.)

✓ Seed ordering charts. (These can be found inside seed catalogs. Students will enter descriptions of the seeds, what size and quantity of packets they will need, and tally up the cost of their order.)

Students observe and record changes caused by decomposition.

Photo by Stephanie Ma

Questions for discussion

» How will we choose what to grow in our garden? What flowers and vegetables grow best here? (Consult your list.) What vegetables do you like to eat? Why are there so many varieties of one vegetable? How can we tell which ones will be the best to grow in our conditions?

» Should we grow seeds for next year's garden? If so, which seeds shall we grow? The ones we choose to grow for seeds must be open-pollinated seeds. Why? What do you think will be the easiest to grow? Fun? Challenging? What season are we planting for, cold or warm? Do we want to choose a variety of edible plant parts—roots, stems, leaves, flowers, fruits, and seeds?

Activity

1. Divide the class into groups of three students.

2. Give each group a copy of the seed ordering chart. Instruct them to fill in the specific characteristics with the answers from the class discussions. Using these characteristics, ask each group to go through their catalog and compile their own list of seeds to grow. Encourage each group to use different criteria, such as variety, cost, and open pollination. (You may want to limit the number of vegetables, flowers, and herbs each group is to select.)

3. As a class, compile one master list of seeds to be ordered and indicate the particular catalog or company to be used.

4. Ask the students in their small groups to fill out an order form for their seed company. Obtain a check or money order and mail it to the company. You might want to combine your order with another class to get a wholesale price. Allow sufficient time for the seeds to arrive.

157

HABITAT RIDDLES

Adapted from Life Lab Science Program (Grade 4, "Habitats"), Santa Cruz, California; www.lifelab.org

Objective

To develop an understanding of how physical conditions affect plant and animal life within a habitat.

Materials

✓ Pictures of diverse habitats (oceans, mountains, and deserts)

✓ Pipe cleaners and other art supplies

✓ Clay

✓ Foil

✓ Toothpicks

Key concepts

» The range of habitats on our planet Earth reflects the diverse combinations of light, temperature, terrain, moisture, elevation, water, and soils; these specific conditions result in a specific type of habitat.

» These conditions are the determining factors in all habitats; even the most exotic environments support life forms that have evolved to meet the most extreme conditions.

» Knowing the physical conditions that generate a habitat offers good clues to some of the features of the plants and animals that live there.

PART 1: GETTING STARTED

Display pictures of diverse habitats: ocean, arctic, tropical forest, prairie, river, and so on. You might use pictures found in magazines, calendars, or other nature books. Describe the specific conditions of each habitat to your students, and chal-

lenge them to match your description to a picture by creating a riddle. For example, you might say: "This habitat is home to plants and animals. On summer days the temperature can soar above 100 degrees (37 C) and then drop to near freezing at night. Winters are mild. Rainfall is scarce and plants grow in scattered clumps in the sandy, dry soil. Many plants have thorns, spines, or tiny leaves and some store water in their fleshy stems. Many of the snakes, lizards, rodents, and other animals that live here burrow in the ground to escape the day's heat. They come out at night or in the cool mornings and evenings to find food. What habitat am I describing?" *Desert.*

Activity

1. Select another habitat picture and have the class use the habitat conditions to make up a riddle. Ask if students can identify any plants and animals in the picture and encourage them to think of how the plants and animals have special features to survive the conditions within that habitat.

2. Divide the class into teams of four to six students. Give each team a picture and have them use it to write a habitat riddle. Remind students not to let other teams see their pictures.

3. After all the groups have finished writing their riddles, collect the pictures and display them so that everyone can see them. Collect the riddles, shuffle them, and pass them out to each team. Let team members confer for a few minutes as they try to match the riddle with its picture.

4. When everyone is ready, select a volunteer from each team to read the riddle and identify the habitat picture that matches it. If the riddle does not have enough clues for students to determine the habitat, ask what other things about the habitat the team needs to know. See if the team that wrote the riddle can supply more clues. If the match is incorrect, compare the similarities

and differences in the right habitat picture with the one chosen. If the information is wrong, ask where the students might find out more about the habitat and help them find references and picture books.

5. Once all the habitats are matched with their pictures, give the teams time to add to, refine, or correct their clues.

6. Display the riddles and pictures so students can match them during their free time.

Assessment

Assess students' understanding of the relationship between physical conditions and habitats:

1. What clues were most helpful for you in solving the habitat riddles?

2. Did clues that named plants and animals help you to identify the habitat?

3. Why do certain animals and plants live in one habitat and not another?

PART 2: GETTING STARTED

Display a picture of an animal within its habitat to discuss how plants and animals use and adapt to their habitats. For example, is the habitat hot or cold, sunny or shady, moist or dry?

Activity

» With habitat pictures on display nearby, ask students to create a plant or animal that could exist in one of these habitats using the pipe cleaners and other art supplies you have provided. What would their animal need to have to survive in the habitat they've chosen?

» Encourage students to think of ways to use the pictures and art supplies to explore habitat conditions and how they influence what lives in a certain place.

» Draw a habitat then challenge a friend to create a plant or animal that lives there.

» Create a plant or animal with special features then challenge a friend to draw a picture of its habitat.

» Join with a team to create a habitat of plants and animals. Use one of the habitat pictures or draw one on your own. What resources do the plants and animals need to find in the habitat?

Follow-up activities

» Encourage students to classify the habitat pictures by light level, temperature, moisture, soil type, or other physical conditions.

» Suggest that students locate different habitats on a globe or map. What relationships are there between geographical location and habitat conditions?

» Use the students' creations to make a diorama of a habitat and the plants and animals that live there. Be sure the habitat supplies the resources that each animal and plant needs.

Borage.

AN INTRODUCTION TO WORM COMPOSTING

Adapted from Jessica Bean, Heather Russell, Kae Bosman-Clark, and others, "Vermicomposting in the Classroom," in the Earth Steward Gardener Curriculum. Copyright © 2007 Cultivating Community, Portland, Maine

Objectives

To give students a better understanding of composting, and to introduce a vermicomposting project to the classroom. Students will learn about both the anatomy of a worm, as well as the worm's amazing abilities to aerate soil and assist in decomposition. They will also learn how to care for worms.

Materials

✓ 1 pound of red worms (maybe you know another gardener who has some to share)

✓ Wooden or plastic bin

✓ Newspaper

✓ Food scraps

✓ Illustration of worm anatomy

Key concepts

» Composting is a way to recycle food.

» Using red wiggler worms is a way to compost food scraps.

» Worms require weekly care to be healthy and make compost.

Discussion

Vermicomposting is a composting process that uses red wiggler worms to break down food scraps and other materials. As the food rots, the worms eat the rotten parts and produce castings, which is really just a fancy word for worm poop, an excellent fertilizer for plants.

Guiding questions

Q: What is recycling?

A: To extract and reuse useful substances found in waste.

Q: What are some things that we usually recycle?

A: Paper, glass, metal, plastic.

Q: What about recycling food waste? How can we do that?

A: Compost!

Q: Why do we want to make compost to amend our soil?

A: Soil health and fertility.

Activity

Begin by introducing the concept of composting as recycling. Most students are familiar with recycling paper, metal, or plastic, but the idea of recycling food waste may be new. Composting can be linked to a lesson on soil health. A quick explanation about the different types of compost may also be appropriate. For example, the most common way of composting is to put food scraps in a pile outside, but they will be focusing on composting with worms (vermicomposting) in this activity.

Next, focus the discussion on the worms themselves. A good way to begin it is to explain the fallacy that when you cut a worm in half, you get two worms. That is not true, and cruelty to worms should not be permitted. Explain that worms have something similar to a brain, a heart, a nervous system, and a digestive system. Ask students what they think a worm needs to live and stay healthy. Food, shelter, water, and air are all essential needs for living things, but for worms, water is impor-

There are many varieties of lettuce.

tant not for drinking but for keeping their skin moist so that gas exchange can occur as they breathe. One can draw the comparison to human lungs, which are also moist to allow oxygen to be exchanged across the membrane.

Assemble the worm bin together in class. Shred the newspaper and place it in the bin. Add food scraps. Evenly moisten the newspaper by sprinkling water over the bin. Then add the worms and a little more newspaper. The bin will need a lid with holes poked in it so that the worms can stay moist and still get oxygen. It is also helpful to have drain holes in the bottom of the bin and a tray beneath it; worms create nutrient-rich moisture as they process the food that can be captured and fed to plants in the classroom. For the first day, leave a light on overnight so that the worms will not want to leave the bin. (They will eventually find the food and stay put.)

Worms need to be fed regularly, but do not overfeed them as the food that they don't eat will rot in the bin and attract pests. They also need a bit of moisture periodically. Check the worms every few days. Their ability to process food will vary depending on the number of worms, their health, and their environment.

How to care for the bins

Once a week check for bedding moisture and food. Things worms like to eat include fruit, vegetables, small amounts of bread, dried and ground-up eggshells. Things not to feed worms: citrus peel, onions, broccoli and its relatives, meat, dairy, or oily foods.

For further reading and lesson plans, look for *Healthy Foods from Healthy Soils* by Elizabeth Patten and Kathy Lyons (Tilbury House 2003) and *The Worm Cafe: A Worm Composting Curriculum Guide* by Binet Payne (Flower Press 1999).

Measuring plant growth.

LAND SCARCITY

Adapted by The San Francisco Green Schoolyard Alliance from *Each A Teacher*, a docent handbook of the Bouverie Audubon Preserve, Sonoma County, California

Objective

To illustrate the scarcity of land available to grow our food and clothing.

Materials

✓ One apple

✓ Knife

Activity

Where do we grow all the plants that eventually become our food? Use an apple to represent the earth. Cut it into quarters. Ask the kids "How much of this earth do you think we have available on which to grow food?" Set aside three of the four quarters. Explain that these are under water.

That leaves one quarter. Cut it in half. Set the other half down and explain that this represents the land that is too mountainous, cold, dry, wet, or otherwise unsuitable for growing food. One eighth of the apple will be left. Cut it into four slices. Explain that three of these slices are already covered by cities and highways. The one tiny piece of the apple that is left over is the amount of the Earth that is capable of producing the food and clothing for billions of people. Hold the tiny portion in your hand and let everyone see just how small it really is.

Discussion

Emphasize the importance of taking care of our land. How do we properly steward our own piece of land, right here at school? We avoid pesticides and other chemicals that pollute our soil and waterways. We amend our beds with compost and keep the soil thriving with life. We are able to grow food for a local food pantry and share the fertility of our soil.

GRAPHING PLANT GROWTH

From the San Francisco Green Schoolyard Alliance

Description

Students create a graph that illustrates a fava bean plant's growth over the season.

Objectives

To illustrate how change over time can be graphically represented, and how graphs can tell a story; to promote observation and a sense of time.

Materials

✓ Fava bean plant seedlings (or other plants, such as peas, that you know will have robust growth over a long period of time)

✓ Large sheet of graph paper (or, make your own graph on poster board)

✓ 1 colored permanent marker

✓ 1 black permanent marker

✓ Straight edge

✓ Tall wooden stake or piece of wood

✓ Popsicle sticks, enough for each student or pair of students

- ✓ Rulers, enough for each student or pair of students
- ✓ Journals
- ✓ Pencils

Getting started

For this activity, you will need several newly germinated fava bean plants or other seedlings that will show robust growth over time, such as peas. Depending on how you want to work with a particular class, you may want to have one plant per student, or divide them up into pairs to determine the number of plants you'll need. The plants can be in pots in the classroom or planted in beds outdoors. Fava beans take seven to fourteen days to germinate, so plant your seeds a week or so ahead—you'll want your seedlings to be at least two centimeters before beginning this unit.

As a class, you will graph the growth of one fava bean plant as a demonstration. Place the wooden stake next to your demonstration plant, and mark the plant's height with your permanent marker regularly to clearly show the change in growth from week to week.

Discussion

Ask students if they notice that any plants have grown. How can we be sure if things have changed? How can we keep track of the growth or decay of our fava bean plants? Discuss the process and principles of measurement and data collection and analysis, and how you will apply these principles in your investigation of the growth of your fava bean plants. Ask students to find out how long it will take a fava bean plant to mature (they can look on their seed packets or research gardening books or Web sites) and then mark on a calendar how long they will be collecting measurements of their plants' growth.

Activity

Tape your large graph paper to the board and use a straight edge to draw the X-axis and Y-axis with the black marker. Label the X-axis "Time" (Date), and label the Y-axis "Height" in centimeters. Place the tall piece of wood in the bed next to the newly germinated plant that you are going to measure.

Have students take a look at the graph you've created. Explain the difference between the X and Y lines with an example of time and height. Point out the stake in the bed. Show how one student will mark where the top of the plant is each week on the stake and measure the height. Each week, you will plot the date and height of the plant with the colored marker. As you go, you will connect the dots (data points) to make a line showing how fast or slow the plant is growing.

What does the graph look like at the end of your period of measurement? What does the line look like? What does that tell you? Did the line descend? What does that mean?

Have each student or pair of students pick their own fava plant to keep track of for a month or however long you decide. Have the students label popsicle sticks with their initials and place them next to their plants. Every week, have students measure the heights of their plants and record the data on graph paper in their journals. At the end of the measurement period, they can graph their results and present their findings to the class.

INTERVIEWING LOCAL FARMERS

Adapted from Jessica Bean, Heather Russell, Kae Bosman-Clark, and others, the Earth Steward Gardener Curriculum. Copyright © 2007 Cultivating Community, Portland, Maine

Objectives

To gain a sense of local agricultural systems, where food comes from, seasonality, and a sense of the work it takes to be a farmer.

Getting started

» Have students prepare for their interviews. A list of questions is provided below. Students should practice these questions in mock interviews with each other: they should be able to formulate these questions clearly, ask appropriate follow-up questions, record results, and respond to an evolving conversation.

» Communicate openly with the farmers who have agreed to partner with you in this exercise. They should be well-informed about what to expect from the interview, and feel comfortable and welcome to bring their own ideas and unique perspectives to the process.

» Plan to make your interviews public in a display, video project, newspaper article, or other venue.

Interview questions

What type of farmer are you? Do you sell anything that you produce?

How did you become interested in farming?

How old is your farm? What is the history of it?

What is a typical day like for you on the farm? How many hours do you work?

What is your favorite thing to do on the farm? What really challenges you?

About how much do you produce and sell in one year? Where or to whom do you sell your product(s)?

What kinds of work do you have to do to grow and harvest your product?

How do you think farming has changed over the years?

Why do you think farming is important?

What are the biggest challenges of farming in today's culture?

Do you use any type of technology on the farm? If so, how?

Do you belong to any farming organizations?

What do you do in your free time? What are your hobbies?

GARDEN SCAVENGER HUNT

From the San Francisco Green Schoolyard Alliance

Objectives

To observe and explore the garden.

Getting started

Students love this activity and it's a great way to quickly test their knowledge of the garden and other relevant subjects like local geography or plant biology. Below is a sample list of questions you might ask during a scavenger hunt. Every garden is different: devise a set of questions that make sense in *your* environment.

Activity

1. Find an aquatic habitat in the garden and name three things that live there:

    1. _____

    2. _____

    3. _____

2. Are there trees that produce fruit in the garden? What are they? Are there any fruit?

3. What local landmark can you see from the garden to the northeast?

4. Find where the mulberry trees are. How many do we have? What eats mulberry leaves? What is the product?

5. Find one yellow flower (name:_____) and sketch it:

6. Find and name three vegetables that we grow in the garden:

    1. _____

    2. _____

    3. _____

7. What street is to the south of the garden?

8. What street is to the east of the garden?

9. In your garden journal, draw a quick map of the garden, showing the four directions. Include: beds, pond, tool shed, seating area, fences, and trees.

10. Check the rain gauge. How much rain have we had recently? _____cm
    What does this say about our region and the season?

POLLUTION SOUP

Adapted by The Watershed Project, Richmond, California

Objectives

To understand how our activities cause urban runoff pollution and impact water quality in creeks and bays. Students will describe how the combined activities of humans have a cumulative effect on our water quality.

Description

Using a jar of water to represent the watershed, students add materials to demonstrate the impact of urban storm water runoff and nonpoint source pollution.

Materials

- ✓ Large, clear container filled with clean water
- ✓ 10 small containers to hold "pollutants" (yogurt containers work well)
- ✓ "Pollutants" to put into the small containers (see "Preparing for the activity," below)

Key concepts

Nonpoint source pollution is caused by the combined actions of individuals who misuse or improperly dispose of common home and garden products.

Background

Our actions at school and home can cause environmental damage to our creeks and waterways. To keep our watersheds healthy, we first need to learn about the effects of our actions, and then how to change our behaviors.

Many people assume that most of our water pollution is caused by large industries and agriculture. This type of pollution is called point source pollution because it can be traced back to one particular source. But the most damaging source of water pollution is actually the combined actions of individuals who misuse, dump, or discard hazardous household substances around their homes, gardens, and city streets. We call this nonpoint source pollution because it is hard to trace the pollution back to just one place.

Antifreeze, oil, insecticides, pesticides, herbicides, household chemicals, fertilizers, paint, and rubber dust from tires are all substances that become pollutants when they are washed off our yards, streets, and parking lots. This polluted water flows into the gutter, disappears down storm drains, flows into creeks, and eventually runs untreated into our waterways.

Getting started

Label each container as follows and fill each with the corresponding "pollutant" materials:

- » "Earth": dirt and rocks
- » "Nature": leaves and twigs
- » "Trash": various wrappers, cigarette butts, etc.
- » "Old Car Owners": molasses or syrup to represent car oil
- » "New Car Owners": liquid soap and water
- » "Just Your Average Car Owners": metal (penny) and rubber (rubber band)
- » "Homeowners": paint
- » "Pet Owners": chocolate covered raisins to represent pet waste
- » "Gardeners": water and green food coloring to represent fertilizers
- » "Industrial Waste": soy sauce and water (use hot water if possible) to represent industrial discharge

9. Year-round Garden Lessons And Activities

Activity

1. Place the "watershed" container (large clear container) where everyone can see it. Ask students if this were a body of water near their home, would they consider swimming in it? Fishing from it? Drinking it?

2. Brainstorm and compile a list of substances that are considered pollutants. Have the students discuss why these materials might contain substances that are harmful to the environment. Ask students to think about how these substances might get into the watershed.

3. Have the class pair or team up into ten groups, one for each of the pollutant groups. Hand out the various containers to the students. Explain that they will be adding potential pollutants to their watershed.

4. Call students up group by group and have them describe what is in their container before emptying the contents into the "watershed."

5. Using the topics and questions grouped below, discuss each pollutant added. Answers to questions are given in italics. With older students, copy the information below and let students ask and answer the questions.

"Earth"

Imagine that there is a heavy rainstorm. Sand, dirt, and pebbles wash from construction sites into the street and then the storm drain. This material ends up in the creeks. Would you still swim, fish, or drink from this water? How might all the debris impact the stream?

Sediment in the water can impact the food chain by decreasing the amount of light available to aquatic plants, increasing the surface temperature of the stream, smothering fish and fish eggs, or by releasing contaminants.

"Nature"

Leaves and other natural debris can get into our storm drains. How might these natural materials pollute our watersheds?

Paved streets and parking lots don't allow organic matter to decompose into soil, and it concentrates in our waterways. Too much debris can block fish migrations, impede water flow, and consume oxygen as it decomposes—reducing the oxygen available for aquatic life.

"Trash"

How might litter end up in the creeks that we cannot even see? How does this impact the health of the creeks?

Litter from far way washes into the creeks and waterways via the storm drain system. Plastics, aluminum, and other human trash does not degrade easily, or contains materials toxic to aquatic life. Would you still swim, fish, or drink from this water?

"Old car owners"

What types of hazardous substances might come from cars?

Copper and asbestos from brakes, rubber from tires, and motor oil are just a few of the by-products of an automobile-based society. One gallon of motor oil can contaminate 250,000 gallons of water. Motor oil contains hydrocarbons and metals that endanger the health of humans and wildlife. Oil creates a film on the surface of water that can smother aquatic animals and coats the feathers of birds, impeding their ability to fly as well as their ability to stay warm and dry. Antifreeze contains ethylene glycol, which is a toxic substance.

"New car owners"

If you had a brand new car, with nice shiny paint, what would you do to take care of it? What goes down the drain with the water when you wash your car? Where does this water go? Why is washing something in the driveway different from washing in the kitchen sink?

Soaps, cleaners, and dirt that go down the drains in your home pass through the water treatment plant before they are flushed to the sea. However, if you wash your car in the driveway or the street, the cleaners enter the storm drain and flow to our creeks and waterways untreated. Phosphates, detergents, and cleaning agents can cause rapid growth of algae, or kill aquatic life outright.

"Just your average car owners"

What do the penny and rubber band in this container represent?

Vehicles may be the single greatest contributor to urban runoff pollution. They are a major source of copper, lead, cadmium, and chromium—all of which are toxic to humans, or aquatic life, or both. Brake pads and tires wear directly onto roads, where the metals and other contaminants can be transported very efficiently into the storm water system, and ultimately into creeks and waterways.

"Homeowners"

What does it look like this container is filled with? What activities of a homeowner might cause pollution?

The container is filled with paint. The solvents used in paint are toxic and flammable. The pigments may contain heavy metals, and many paints contain fungicides to inhibit mold growth. When leftover paint is poured down the storm drain, or brushes and rollers are cleaned outside, our watershed is polluted.

Watering the garden.

"Pet owners"

How does pet waste get into the watershed? What impact can pet or human waste have?

Pet owners who don't pick up after their pets allow waste and the bacteria and parasites it carries to enter the watershed. Fecal coliforms and E. coli bacteria contamination make water unsafe for swimming and drinking.

"Gardeners"

How many products can you think of that we apply to our gardens and landscapes? If they are applied to plants, how might they end up as runoff into our creeks?

Pesticides, herbicides, fertilizers, and weed killers are just a few of the products commonly used by gardeners that contain hazardous chemicals. Many of these products are washed into our storm drains and on to creeks and bays by over watering or rain water. Many of the ingredients in pesticides and herbicides are toxic to aquatic life. The nutrients in fertilizers can cause algal bloom, which consumes the oxygen in the water, suffocating aquatic life.

"Industrial waste"

How is the waste from industry different from the waste from our homes?

While there is more regulation of industrial pollution then home pollution, some industries illegally dump toxic waste or discharge hot water into rivers and waterways. Industrial toxins are equally as harmful as the toxins in our homes; and temperature changes from hot water can quickly kill aquatic life.

Follow-up activities

» Let the "watershed" container sit for all to see. Discuss the lessons that can be learned from this demonstration. Explain that environmental scientists think in terms of point source and nonpoint source pollution. Nonpoint source pollution does not come from a single, identifiable place, but is rather the accumulation from a variety sources. All but one of the sources above are generally considered nonpoint source pollution, or urban runoff in this case. (Agricultural runoff is another source of nonpoint source pollution.) Can you figure out which one is usually a type of point source pollution? *Industrial waste. While you can make the argument that each thing by itself is a point source of pollution, all are flushed from many locations into creeks and waterways through the storm drain system and collectively are nonpoint source pollutants.*

» For younger students: draw a picture of a healthy watershed.

» For older students: write about urban runoff

pollution in our community. Allow students to choose a creative writing or essay format.

Questions for discussion

1. Describe the watershed in the container. Would this water be safe to drink? To swim in? For wildlife?

2. How can these pollutants get into creeks and waterways?

3. Who is responsible for polluting the water?

4. Which of the sources of pollution did you know about? Which ones didn't you know about?

5. Were any of the activities that cause pollution things you or your family might do?

6. Who should be responsible for cleaning up the water?

7. What can individuals do to lessen the problem of nonpoint source pollution?

Branching out

» Provide students with a variety of "clean up" materials (coffee filters, scoops, fish nets, spoons, wire mesh, cheesecloth, funnels, paper towels, gravel, charcoal, etc.) and ask them to try and filter out the impurities in the water.

» Walk around your school and look for storm drains and pollution.

» Take a field trip to a local creek and look for storm drain outflow pipes and other sources of pollution. Make a visual survey of the health of the creek.

» Take a field trip to the local sewage treatment plant.

» Have students do further research on each of the examples of pollution used in this activity and present to the class.

Discovering a new bird's nest.
Photo by Stephanie Ma

A DECADE IN A SCHOOL GARDEN

Alice Fong Yu Alternative School, San Francisco, California

Recounting the transformation of a school garden project over time, from a germ of an idea into a mature and vibrant program in an inner city school makes a great story. As the founding parent and first garden coordinator at Alice Fong Yu Alternative School in San Francisco, we have unique perspectives on the process of growing a school garden from the ground up. This chapter follows one school through a decade of challenges and triumphs, included here to shed light on the processes of keeping a garden program vital, changing, and sustained over time.

Students celebrate and enjoy a snack in the garden.

Garden signs are in Chinese and English.

ARDEN: REFLECTIONS OF A FOUNDING PARENT

Alice Fong Yu Alternative School Garden Program began as a scrappy patch of vegetables on a windy dune in San Francisco's Inner Sunset District. Over the past twelve years it has grown to include a pond with a solar-powered pump, a native plant area, copious vegetable beds, and various composting systems; and it has helped countless young people understand their natural world. Alice Fong Yu is the nation's first public Chinese-language immersion school. Originally in a shabby old brick building housing kindergarten through fifth grades, the school has been renovated and made fully accessible for the handicapped, and expanded to include grades six, seven, and eight.

School principal Liana Szeto is the mastermind behind the school. The immersion program began as a strand of a neighboring school, but quickly gained traction and was moved to its own site. Liana is a Chinese American originally from the concrete jungle of Hong Kong. She and her family emigrated to the United States when she was a teenager, and she went on to study Environmental Studies at the University of California at Berkeley. She has an unusual blend of steely resolve and openness to new ideas.

Students at Alice Fong Yu, who come from all ethnic and racial backgrounds, begin kindergarten with a teacher who speaks only Cantonese in the classroom. By the end of September, kindergarten students are singing songs and counting in Chinese, writing Chinese characters, and performing small skits. English language arts are also introduced of course. By the time the students are graduating from fifth grade their Cantonese is good, their English is above average, and they are ready to take on Mandarin Chinese in middle school. In one short decade, Alice Fong Yu Alternative School has joined the ranks of San Francisco's highest-performing schools.

There is something about the rigorous academics inside the classrooms and the more free-floating activities in the garden at Alice Fong Yu that provides a unique kind of synergy. Students learn how to sit quietly in their classrooms, but they also learn how to dig up to their elbows in dirt to harvest new potatoes.

When I was a new kindergarten parent, I was surprised by the lack of play opportunities for students on the yard. It was a typical half acre of blacktop with some faded lines and ragged basketball hoops and a long wall suitable for playing suicide (a ball game). Eventually a play structure was added, but it was either windy and cold or hot and glaring on that yard.

Above the yard, on a steep sandy slope was an entirely empty open dune, almost a half a city block in size. Some neighbors took care of the space; others deposited their car doors, batteries and dead cats on the dune. It was covered in green grass in the springtime, which dried to a uniform brown in summer. Many people walked their dogs there, making no effort to pick up after them. This uncolonized urban space accommodated such a variety of creatures: meadowlarks skulked through the grasses looking for insects, cats pounced on gophers, gophers continually moved sand from deep in the earth to the surface, neighbors sat in the sun, sharp-shinned hawks scanned for songbirds, and a kestrel ate his share of Jerusalem crickets. Even the San Francisco zookeeper sometimes roamed the dune to harvest eucalyptus branches for the koala bears.

I found out that the dune was owned by our school district, and also discovered some degree of infrastructure—namely a hose bibb. Armed with this information I approached the principal and suggested that a garden might be a great addition to the school. She was game to try. At that time, the school was so new that there were not a lot of competing programs, and it seemed a great way to add some outdoor richness into the life of the students. We procured a small amount of money from the parent association ($500) to purchase some timber and fencing. A workday was organized and parents hungry for ways to participate in their new school came in droves. On that first workday we assembled raised beds, installed a suggestion of a fence, moved soil into the beds, and were ready to begin. What exactly we were going to begin was unclear. As we had not engaged in any planning (who knew?) there was

Lessons often take place around the center table. *Photo by Stephanie Ma*

no vision on how the new garden was going to be used. There was no notion of the teachers using the garden for teaching themselves. Most of our teachers had grown up in Hong Kong, and had no idea how to engage kids in the outdoors. That was evident by the elegant high heels so many teachers wore to the garden at first. ("Good for soil aerating," I would mutter under my breath watching each stiletto disappear into the soft dirt). Liana, never one to waste a second of possible instructional time, took me aside and suggested that I teach garden classes. She pulled together a few thousand dollars as a modest stipend and I began.

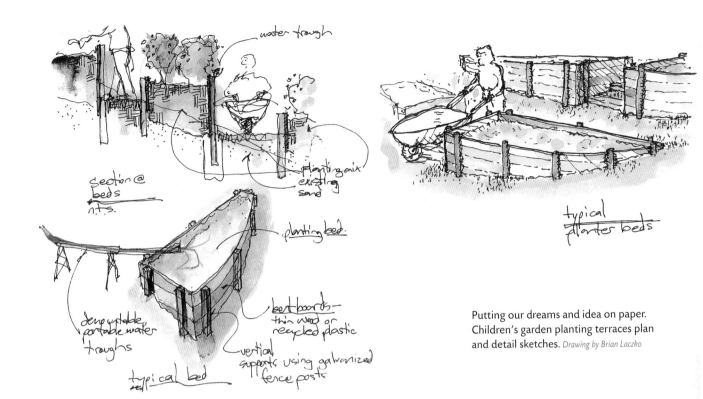

water trough

section @ beds n.t.s.

planting mix @ existing sand

planting bed.

typical bed

best boards— thin wood or recycled plastic

vertical supports using galvanized fence posts

demountable portable water troughs

typical planter beds

Putting our dreams and idea on paper. Children's garden planting terraces plan and detail sketches. *Drawing by Brian Laczko*

Those first years were utter trial and error. I understood kids, having three boys of my own, but managing large numbers of kids in the garden, and actually *teaching* involved a steep learning curve. Liana was a great help, and her belief in the project continued to move it forward. It never occurred to me to find out if other schools were engaged in similar projects and programs. Indeed they were, and I would have saved myself a lot of time and hassle if I had known.

Challenges aside, those first years of the program were golden. The students were so electrified by the garden: planting, nurturing, harvesting, eating, weeding, finding interesting bugs, and getting acquainted with all the creatures that called the dune home. The teachers loved it; it was impossible to deny how much the kids loved to be outside, how happy they were in the garden, and how much more willing they were to settle down when they returned to the classroom. The parents loved the garden and supported it financially, and willingly invested their time and sweat and expertise. Over time, the garden began to look less casual and took on the features that turned it into a real classroom. We asked a parent to dissect a cypress trunk into twenty kid-sized rounds and made an outdoor classroom. We mounted a whiteboard on a wall for the teachers to use, and we purchased clipboards and a tool shed. Small amounts of grant money were raised each year to further support the program. We were constantly finding ways to make the garden more relevant to the school day. The school was gaining in popularity, as more and more parents became intrigued with the opportunity for their children to absorb Chinese at such an early age. Before we knew it, it was time to expand the footprint of the school, and the logical option was to build it right on top of the new garden.

The garden was in a vulnerable position. The school was going to expand; there was no avoiding the fact that it had to expand right into the garden space. If the garden program lay fallow for a couple of years during the construction, could it be restarted? Fortunately, the San Francisco Botanical Garden in Golden Gate Park was looking for ways to deepen its relationship with the public school system, and Alice Fong Yu students were the perfect pioneer gardeners. Rather than heading out to the school garden every week, the students from each grade level walked to the nearby botanical garden twice a semester to spend an entire morning working in the children's garden. We tinkered with curriculum, appropriate grade level instruction, and programmatic elements to hone the children's program at the botanical garden. The instructors were impressed with the knowledge our students already had about their environment, general botany, and stewardship of plants. For two years we were able to expand the garden program into a more comprehensive environmental education program, thanks to the resources of the botanical garden. In that fifty-five acre public garden in the middle of San Francisco, students were able to visit deep redwood forests and open oak savannahs, grind acorns in bedrock mortars, see California wildflowers in bloom, and maintain the vegetable garden.

In the meantime, we were offered a new garden site at Alice Fong Yu. It was a steep northwest-facing slope at the top of the dune, dotted with several mature trees. The district agreed to provide fencing for the new garden site, which we greatly appreciated. The problem was how to deal with the slope, and how to turn the site into a teaching garden.

Clearly our sophistication had increased. By now, we had a well-established garden committee, with many people of varying skills willing to dig in. One of our members helped with grant writing, another knew how to drive an excavator, another put us in touch with an architect to help us figure out how to make the most out of a very sloped site. The committee had taken field trips to other Bay Area school gardens, and we had clear goals and objectives. We met frequently, developed a plan, hired the architect to make drawings, and presented them to the parent association, principal, and teachers for their input. As a garden coordinator with a bit of experience (finally), I was able to develop a document describing which standards were being met in the garden, what curriculum was being used, and how we planned to continue to develop and fund the program. We wrote articles in the school newspaper, we took over a centrally located bulletin board, and we started an annual garden party tradition. Liana and I spoke periodically and brainstormed ideas on how to deepen the connections between teachers and the garden. Now that we had a middle school, we started a community service component in the garden. This was going to be "Alice Fong Yu School Garden 2.0," and we were excited to build on the knowledge we had gained from the last garden.

This was a period of great growth in the broader Bay Area school garden movement. Fueled in part by Alice Waters' Edible Schoolyard and the copious press it was receiving, suddenly almost everyone had heard of this great idea called school gardens. In San Francisco an organization called the San Francisco Green Schoolyard Alliance was beginning to make itself known. A central hub for information on school gardens, the new organization published periodic resources and opportunities for professional development for teachers and garden coordinators, which caused a surge in the local movement. The Growing Greener School Grounds Conference was established in 2002 , bringing together teachers and school garden practitioners from all over the Bay Area for hands-on workshops in three district schools. A voter approved school district bond for Americans with Disabilities Act upgrades was passed that allocated funding for developing green schoolyards and school gardens.

Alice Fong Yu was ready to move forward with another garden coordinator. This period of time, when the founding parent steps aside is a vulnerable time for a garden project. Happily, Rachel, the new coordinator, and those who have followed her, have been well mentored by the principal. While every garden coordinator has their own interests and motivations, they have each continued to deepen and strengthen the connections to the classroom and maintained the relevance of the program.

Sometimes the benches become convenient desks. *Photo by Stephanie Ma*

RACHEL: REFLECTIONS OF A GARDEN COORDINATOR

I came on as the next garden coordinator at Alice Fong Yu after Arden left to help further the school garden movement within San Francisco Unified School District. With a background in environmental education and farming, the mix between the two in school gardens was ideal. But it was not without trepidation that I began taking over the project that so many parents had poured their sweat and hearts into. I was the outsider, but young and willing. After I was hired, I attended the first staff meeting of the year to introduce myself and to set up a schedule for garden classes. The job was part time and I was wondering how I would make a living in San Francisco on what would be $18,000 a year. The teachers wanted to have garden class in the afternoons, from about 1:00 p.m. until the end of the day at 3:30. I was to oversee lunch in the garden, as well. So my job would be from noon until school ended; I would either look for work at after-school programs or get another part-time job in the mornings. Eventually, I filled out my hours at Alice Fong Yu as a literacy tutor in the mornings for kindergarten and first grades. Incidentally, this work allowed me to get to know the students and parents at the school to a greater degree than would have been possible just through the garden. It also afforded me an opportunity to become acquainted with the curriculum that was being used and the concepts being covered in class; and I would try to echo and enhance those concepts in the garden.

Building on what Arden and the other parents had started, I met with teachers at their grade level meetings and got a sense of their "scope and sequence" for the year. For instance, kindergarten teachers would be covering their "seeds and weeds" unit in October. I would design new or use existing curriculum that also covered these general concepts during that month. I worked to be consistent, teaching in the garden everyday, and when it was rainy, taking lessons inside.

The Alice Fong Yu School Garden is primarily a food-systems garden. With fifteen raised beds, there was plenty of room to grow vegetables. Instead of assigning a bed to each class, which is sometimes a good way to focus student observation, the garden beds belonged to all of the classes. We sowed beds of carrots, lettuces, chard, and fava beans, among others. We produced food. And we ate it. I brought my small backpacking stove and a large wok to the garden. We'd harvest chard and sauté it with onions and garlic and olive oil and snack on this during class. We'd do the same with broccoli, collards, and a number of other greens. Sometimes I would make pasta beforehand and add this to our sautés. We crushed fresh peas with pumpkin seeds and garlic and olive oil in our mortar and pestles for a dip that we ate with crackers. Eventually, we graduated from my finicky backpacking stove to a one-burner butane stove that turned on just like a gas range. It could simmer (something my old stove would not do)!

After four years as the garden educator and coordinator at Alice Fong Yu, the garden was fully accepted into the schedule as a vital program at the school. Nevertheless, there was the ongoing work of making the classes relevant to the teachers and the education standards and convincing teachers that garden time wasn't simply free time, but instructional time. Some teachers eventually entrusted me with entire units that they wanted to cover, and they discovered that they could use garden-time to get to them. (For example, we covered "Landforms" each year in the garden, a fourth grade science unit.) Some teachers were never willing to relinquish control over some standards that could have been easily taught in the garden, preferring to teach them inside. We also had our ebb and flow of garden committee members and interested parents. Each year we worked to recruit new members—new kindergarten parents who would take up the charge of supporting the garden. This was not always an easy task. But this ebb and flow of enthusiasm was a natural process and new projects in the garden always awakened a refreshed spirit. Never "finishing" the garden was important, as ongoing improvement projects kept parents interested and invested.

Before leaving Alice Fong Yu, I created a guide called "Garden Coordinator's Handbook." In it I put the yearly school picture of all the teachers and their names. I copied and filed old lessons. I left a new lesson plan book along with my old ones with all my notes on what was covered and when. I wrote an introduction to the position, what to expect, who at the school was in charge of what, and how the garden program ran in general. When I first came on as garden coordinator, as a young college graduate having had no children of my own, I was not privy to the workings of an elementary school: how parents were involved, what the Parents Association did, and what all the education standards were. I knew a little, but it took some time for me to understand my role in the school. The garden was not everyone's central focus, as it was mine. The school garden needed to be continuously woven into the fabric of the school and I needed to spearhead that process. In my letter to the new garden educator, I explained their role and how to not only survive, but to thrive and to not be afraid to take the garden to the next level. Subsequently, Alice Fong Yu has had two more garden educators, Fiona and Stephanie, and they each have brought their own spirit and talents to the position. Each transition has occurred relatively smoothly, as the school continues to support and believe in the program.

San Francisco Mayor Gavin Newsom visiting a SFUSD garden.

These urbanite beds on the schoolyard are just the beginning.

STARTING A LOCAL MOVEMENT

An individual school garden program is fragile, dependent on ongoing parent enthusiasm and support, principal and teacher engagement, and a clear and sturdy organizational plan. When school garden programs band together and speak with one voice, they become a force to be reckoned with. In our school district, we had identified twenty-eight different school gardens with garden coordinators doing the herculean job of teaching, fundraising, curriculum-building, and promoting their school gardens. We knew that providing teachers, parents, and garden coordinators with an opportunity to communicate and develop relationships with one another was a first step in building a larger movement. We organized casual social networking events and asked parents and coordinators to share their successes and challenges. We created an easy to use list-serv, and the school district offered a central location for useful and free resources to school gardens. Offering free garden materials, such as easily accessible compost, mulch, and seedlings drew in even the most independent-minded garden coordinators who otherwise might have been reluctant to become part of something bigger. While individual schools were able to beg or buy these materials, we had great success in asking suppliers to donate large quantities of materials, which we stored at a central location. In addition, we found and circulated all funding opportunities, and helped parents and garden coordinators write their first grants.

Matching new garden programs with more established ones allowed a mentoring program to flourish. Finally, organizing visits with dignitaries or elected officials to garden sites developed fierce school pride in the program and helped spread the word of environmental and garden-based education.

We suggested that school garden programs would benefit from a district-wide coordinator to understand what school gardens need to survive from year to year, and help them do it. The district was willing to provide office space and whatever support they could, although funding is always in short supply. Grant funding was located for salary support, and the position of director of educational gardens was established. Interestingly, this small step proved to be surprisingly far-reaching, as a district position indicated administrative support, and this positive attitude radiated out to principals and other school administrators. Principals called to find out how their sites could have a garden program.

Our district now has more than eighty school gardens. Seven million dollars has now been allocated for design and construction of forty-five green schoolyards in our district, a very small portion of the overall modernization bond that will eventually bring half of the SFUSD schools into ADA (Americans with Disabilities Act) compliance and upgrade the facilities of so many of our historic city schools. The San Francisco Green Schoolyard Alliance has been instrumental in guiding the greening portion of the bond program, which allows school sites to envision and implement their own greening dreams and to develop strategies for sustaining them. With funding in the range of $150,000 dollars per school site, the bond program has offered schools an excellent start for building their outdoor classroom and making their site more beautiful and environmentally appealing.

The bond management department has hatched an ingenious process for supporting schools as they develop their green spaces. All sites must undergo a lengthy decision-making process involving the entire community; as a result decisions about what greening elements each site would like is almost entirely decided by the teachers, parents, students, and administration of that particular site. The bond department manages the complex process of developing drawings and contracts. The happy consequence of imagining, articulating, building, and sustaining a green schoolyard or school garden is of course a stronger, more engaged school community.

A victory garden was installed for the summer in front of our city hall. California's First Lady Maria Shriver championed an assembly bill that allocated fifteen million dollars to school gardens in our state. Michelle Obama spoke in front of five hundred service volunteers in

Sunflowers attract pollinators and are a cheerful addition to a school garden.

a SFUSD green schoolyard about the importance of eating fresh vegetables and going outside to play. Our mayor and board of supervisors are fervent supporters of local food systems and urban agriculture. It is logical that school gardens play a part in this enormous groundswell of interest in growing and eating locally grown fruits and vegetables. None of this would have been possible had we been a disparate group of individual school gardens. The unified and organized structure we have put into place allows us to participate in the school garden movement on a much larger scale.

We continue to grow and change as we confront challenges, cutbacks, and navigate the shifting sands of public education, policy, and civic interest. We believe that a change is occurring in our public schools, and for whatever reason, parents are bravely and resolutely engaging to improve their schools and make them work.

Daniel Webster Elementary school was on the chopping block for the second time. It was underenrolled and the district was making painful funding cuts everywhere, and couldn't afford to keep it open. A band of young neighborhood parents hoped to be able to send their kids there and organized to protest the cuts and keep the doors open. Not only were they successful, they went on to raise nearly a half a million dollars to build a preschool on the site, which would hopefully feed the elementary school. Now, five years later, their kindergarten-aged children are entering the Spanish immersion program at Daniel Webster. They have built gardens all around the school site and sidewalk and are interested in hiring a garden coordinator. They have planted trees, which are tended by neighbors in the summer. Most striking, however, is that the school now has a waiting list of neighborhood parents clamoring to get their children in and be a part of this remarkable transformation.

WHERE DO WE GO FROM HERE?

Observing the interest in school gardens over the past century, one cannot help but be impressed by the number of times they have been used as a teaching tool in schools around the world. If one were to plot the resurgence of school garden interest on a graph from the late 1800s to current times, it would be a consistently undulating wave of

Clipboards make great portable desks.

peaks followed by valleys. School gardens and garden-based education, while enjoying periods of great popularity, have never made it into mainstream education. In their paper on garden-based learning prepared for the Food and Agriculture Organization of the United Nations, Desmond, Greishop, and Subramanian suggest that a garden-based "pedagogy has not been critically examined and endorsed by educational researchers and practitioners." That is not to say that research conducted on the efficacy of school gardens doesn't exist, but its use in solidifying the school garden as a universally accepted teaching tool has not happened. Also, "there is no developed discipline in garden-based learning that makes the connection . . . to advancement in academic performance." Simply stated, there is "no consistent framework within which to apply the pedagogy" (Desmond, Greishop, and Subramanian 2003). Additionally, there is little or no exposure to garden-based learning or environmental education in teachers' colleges as they train new inductees into the profession. And particularly in urban settings, there are simply fewer gardeners amongst the teaching population to carry the torch.

Finally, if outdoor classrooms were an accepted and supported part of school infrastructure and budgeted for accordingly just like all other classrooms and site facilities, sustainability would naturally follow. Also, as school librarians are trained in the management of a library, garden coordinators could be trained in environmental education and garden-based learning to work with classroom teachers to design or develop environmental and garden-based curriculum and deliver it to students. These strategies for mainstreaming school gardens will require more research and hard data (rather than the anecdotal data that abounds) to convince education policy makers to seriously consider this shift.

The great migration away from farms and rural life to cities that occurred in the 1940s and 50s has now separated two generations from ongoing exposure to the natural world and agricultural systems. Often students will tell of their experiences of planting in a backyard garden with their grandmother or grandfather, but rarely will we hear of this experience with their parents. As the link between humans and our own ecology becomes more and more tenuous, we have the opportunity to strengthen and rebuild those connections in a school garden before they become too distant to be relevant.

Students spend six to eight hours a day at their school, which makes it a logical place for them to develop relationships not only with their teachers and peers, but also with the natural systems that are found in the school garden.

SCHOOL GARDEN RECIPES

Cooking in the garden with students is simple and fun. As your school garden grows and evolves, you will undoubtedly come up with your own favorite recipes to share with each other. All of the following recipes are easy for students to follow and simple to prepare. Most quantities are scaled for a class of twenty to thirty students and are intended to be tasty and nutritious snacks, not entire meals. Certain ingredients have not been given specific quantities, as you will discern how much or little you require based on your needs (such as salad greens, crackers, or tortilla chips). A class full of hungry seventh graders will eat a lot more than kindergarteners. Don't worry if garden time follows lunchtime, students will always be hungry for vegetables they have grown and harvested themselves.

Keeping your cooking kit well-stocked in your garden's tool shed will make all of your cooking activities run more smoothly. You will need all of the basic tools and pantry staples mentioned in chapter 8, "Planting, Harvesting, and Cooking in the Garden" to prepare these recipes. Occasionally you may need to plan ahead to bring in some special equipment or ingredients from home, but most often everything you need can come straight from your garden!

THE RECIPES

Herb and Edible Flower Salad	186
Tamari Dijon Salad Dressing	186
Lemon Olive Oil Dressing	187
Basic Stir Fry	188
Honey Lemon Sauté	188
Fresh Pea, Pumpkin Seed, and Garlic Dip	189
Edible Flower Canapés	191
Scissor Salsa	191
Sun-Oven Roasted Potatoes	192
Pasta with Garlicky Greens	192
Lemon Verbena Raspberry Sorbet	193
Fresh Apples and Local Cheeses	194

Basic kitchen tools to include in your garden's cooking kit:

- » *Camping stove, single-burner (or any portable stove that is easy to use and powerful enough to boil water)*
- » *Wok (not electric)*
- » *Tongs*
- » *Salad spinner*
- » *Glass jar with tight-fitting lid for salad dressings*
- » *Large wooden spoons*
- » *A couple of big serving bowls*
- » *Several small prep bowls*
- » *Knives and cutting boards*
- » *2 or 3 mortars and pestles*
- » *Several large buckets for washing hands, greens, and dishes*
- » *Reusable plates and forks for 20–30 students*
- » *Dish soap and clean dish towels*

HERB AND EDIBLE FLOWER SALAD

Any downtown restaurant would be proud to serve a salad as colorful and fresh as this one. It combines fresh greens and lettuces, vibrant petals from edible flowers, such as borage, nasturtium, and calendula, and a few freshly picked herbs from whatever you have on hand. The amount of greens you harvest will depend on the class size and age of the students. If you have each student harvest their own portion—a handful of four or five medium-sized leaves—you will likely have the correct amount of salad for your feast. Lessen the number of leaves for kindergartners. Kids love to pick and eat flowers. Have each student pick one or two flowers of their choosing to add to the dressed salad. You can use any homemade dressing, including the two we offer here.

Ingredients

Fresh lettuce greens
Fresh edible flowers, such as nasturtium, calendula, borage
Fresh herbs, chopped

Harvest, wash and dry enough lettuce greens for the class you will be serving, along with a bunch of edible flowers and a handful of any herbs you might be growing in your garden. Chop the herbs and toss with the greens and flowers. Drizzle with your favorite dressing, then toss again and serve.

TAMARI DIJON SALAD DRESSING

Kids love this tangy, easy to make dressing! If you are using store-bought dressing on freshly grown and harvested organic salad greens, you need to have your head examined! Many students (and parents) don't know how easy it is to make a dressing from scratch.

This recipe will yield about 2 cups of dressing and will be enough for a huge salad for twenty hungry fourth graders.

Ingredients

1 cup apple cider vinegar
1 heaping tablespoon Dijon mustard
¼ cup tamari

Fresh greens!

4 garlic cloves, pressed
Small handful dried or chopped fresh herbs
Juice of one lemon if you have it in the garden (optional, but it
    brightens the flavor)
½ cup olive oil
Ground pepper (no salt—the tamari is salty enough!)

Combine everything but the olive oil in a jar with a tightly fitting
lid and shake vigorously. Be sure to have students do the measuring.
Add oil and shake well. Pour over salad leaves and toss gently. Dressing will keep for several days in the fridge if you have extra.

LEMON OLIVE OIL DRESSING

Even easier, this simple dressing can be made in seconds. If you live in a
warm climate where citrus can grow, think about planting a lemon, lime,
or orange tree in your garden. Fruit trees make excellent additions to
the garden for many reasons, but especially for cooking.

Ingredients

¼ cup olive oil
2–3 fresh lemons
Salt to taste

Special equipment

Lemon juicer (if you have one)

Prepare freshly harvested, washed, and dried garden greens in a big
bowl. Drizzle olive oil and sprinkle salt over greens and toss gently.
When leaves are uniformly coated with oil, squeeze lemon juice over
the leaves and toss, and serve.

BASIC STIR-FRY

Stir-fries are extremely easy to do in the garden. Use whatever produce is ready to harvest and add noodles. Cellophane noodles are quick and easy to prepare. They can be found in the ethnic foods section of most grocery stores, but if you have trouble finding them, any long pasta such as udon noodles, spaghetti, or linguini will do, but will require some extra preparation.

Ingredients

2 or 3 (14-ounce) packages of cellophane noodles
2 tablespoons olive oil
4 cloves garlic, chopped
1 medium onion, chopped
2–3 carrots, chopped
3 bunches of fresh greens, such as kale, chard, or collards, chopped
Handful of snap peas
¼ cup soy sauce

Prior to class, heat 2 quarts of water and pour into a bowl over cellophane noodles and let sit. In class, heat olive oil in wok over stove and add garlic and onions. Cook until translucent. Add carrots and cook for another 2 minutes. Add greens and peas and cook until greens have wilted. Drain cellophane noodles and add them to the wok, stirring to mix with the vegetables. Once noodles are heated thoroughly, turn off heat and toss with soy sauce. Serve.

HONEY LEMON SAUTÉ

This is another version of a stir-fry, but uses a little honey to cut the bitterness of the greens. You can also add other produce that may be ready to pick.

Ingredients

2 tablespoons olive oil
1 medium onion, chopped
3–4 bunches of fresh greens, such as kale, chard, collards, chopped
Salt to taste

Juice of one lemon
2 heaping tablespoons of honey
1 fresh baguette, sliced for 20 or 30

Heat olive oil in wok over stove. Add onions and cook until translucent. Add greens and salt and cook until the greens have sufficiently wilted. Stir in lemon juice and honey; and cook until greens are coated. Turn off heat and serve with fresh bread.

FRESH PEA, PUMPKIN SEED, AND GARLIC DIP

If you don't have a mortar and pestle in your garden, go get two or three of these useful outdoor kitchen tools. This easy-to-make dip is just one of many recipes that involves simply mashing ingredients together. Makes approximately 6 cups of dip.

Ingredients

4 cups fresh shelled peas, parboiled
3 cloves garlic
2 cups dry-roasted pumpkin seeds (pepitas)
¼ cup olive oil
Salt to taste
Crackers for dipping

Parboil the peas prior to class. Divide garlic among mortar and pestles and mash. Add a cup or so of the peas and continue to mash. Add ½ cup of the pumpkin seeds to each and mash well. Add roughly one tablespoon of olive oil to marry the ingredients. Continue to add the rest of the peas, seeds, and a little oil and salt until you have a consistent texture. Scoop into a few dipping bowls and serve with crackers.

Edible Flower Canapés.

Scissor Salsa.

EDIBLE FLOWER CANAPÉS

We first learned this recipe from Laurel Anderson at Salmon Creek School in Occidental California. These are beautiful and exotic, and kids love to eat them. They are particularly attractive and festive at a garden party. This recipe makes enough for just one or two canapés per student, so double it if you'd like to serve them more.

Ingredients

20–30 fresh edible flowers from the garden, such as calendula, borage, nasturtium
Whole grain crackers
2 (8-ounce) containers of cream cheese, or another sticky spread for crackers

Pick a basket of edible flowers, and clean all stems from them. Spread crackers with cream cheese (or any other sticky spread that you may prefer). Arrange brightly colored flowers on top and serve.

SCISSOR SALSA

Scissor Salsa is another favorite from Laurel Anderson of Salmon Creek School. This is a great recipe that lots of kids can participate in and requires no knife skills.

Ingredients

8 cups cherry tomatoes
1 bunch cilantro
8 green onions
4 cloves garlic
Juice of one lime
Salt to taste
Tortilla chips

Special equipment

20–30 pairs of clean child-size scissors

Have students cut tomatoes, cilantro, and onion with scissors into small bowls. Peel, then crush the garlic with a mortar and pestle. Combine all ingredients in a larger bowl. Add lime juice and a little salt. Serve with tortilla chips.

SUN-OVEN ROASTED POTATOES

This is a quick and easy snack and an excellent lesson on the sun's incredible energy.

Ingredients

8–10 small new potatoes or 3–4 small sweet potatoes
Salt and pepper to taste
2 tablespoons olive oil

Special equipment

Sun oven

In the morning, place your oven in the sun, put potatoes inside, and close the lid tightly. Throughout the day, turn the oven to maximize the heat production and check the thermometer reading with your students who are in the garden throughout the day. When it reaches 200–300 degrees, the potatoes should be ready in a couple of hours, but keep checking. When they are soft to the touch, they are done cooking. Cut them into smaller pieces and toss with a little olive oil, salt, and pepper if desired, and serve.

PASTA WITH GARLICKY GREENS

If kids weren't sure how to identify the flavor of garlic before these greens, they will know after you serve this easy sauté.

Ingredients

1 or 2 (16-ounce) packages of penne pasta
2 tablespoons olive oil
3–4 bunches of fresh greens, such as kale, chard, or collards
4–5 cloves of garlic, chopped
Salt to taste

Cook the pasta prior to class and have on hand. During class, heat olive oil in wok over stove. Add garlic, and cook until slightly browned. Add greens one bunch at a time and sprinkle with salt, stirring to coat the leaves in oil. When the greens have wilted, add the pasta and heat through. Serve.

LEMON VERBENA AND RASPBERRY SORBET

This is another recipe from Laurel Anderson of Salmon Creek School. The flavors of lemon verbena and raspberry are incredible—parents and students will want to know how you were able to make this crowd-pleasing treat. This recipe will make about one quart of sorbet, so you may want to double it if you have a large class.

Depending on your climate, you may be able to grow various types of edible berries in your school garden. Raspberries, blackberries, or even blueberries are a great pick-at-will crop, or when the opportunity arises, delicious in recipes such as this one. If you are unable to grow berries in your own garden, there may be a "pick-your-own" farm nearby that would make for a fun and educational field trip.

Ingredients

2 cups white sugar
2 cups water
Handful fresh lemon verbena leaves
2 cups fresh raspberries (or frozen if fresh berries aren't available)
Rock salt and ice for the ice cream maker (see manufacturer's
   instructions for quantities)

Special equipment

Hand-crank ice cream maker
Blender

Make a simple syrup by boiling the sugar in the water until all the sugar has dissolved . Add a handful of lemon verbena leaves to the solution, and let it steep and cool for about 15 minutes. Remove the leaves. Blend raspberries and simple syrup. Pack the hand-crank ice cream maker with rock salt and ice. Pour the combined ingredients into the canister and crank away.

FRESH APPLES AND LOCAL CHEESES

This recipe is really a suggestion for polishing off a few of the many apples that you will have in the garden with a thriving apple tree. Select a few cheeses from local farms and show students how to pair flavors by eating a slice of apple topped with a slice of cheese.

Explain how cheese not only comes from cow's milk, but that it can also be made with sheep and goat milk, and you can taste the difference! Apples and cheese makes a delicious and easily prepared snack.

Ingredients

10–15 apples from the garden, cut into pieces (enough for half an apple per student)
Sampling of kid-friendly local cheeses, cut into small slices (cheese from a variety of animals is best: goat, sheep, and cow)

Special equipment

Cheese knife

On one of the cutting boards, cut the apples into slices and discard the seeds. On the other cutting board, display and slice the different cheeses. Top the apple slices with cheese and sample.

EXAMPLE OF STATE CONTENT STANDARDS

Excerpted from California State Content Standards,
www.cde.ca.gov/be/st/ss/documents/sciencestnd.pdf

KINDERGARTEN: LIFE SCIENCE STANDARD 2

Different types of plants and animals inhabit the earth. As a basis for understanding this concept:

✓ Students know how to observe and describe similarities and differences in the appearance and behavior of plants and animals (for example, seed-bearing plants, birds, fish, insects).

✓ Students know stories sometimes give plants and animals attributes they do not really have.

✓ Students know how to identify major structures of common plants and animals (for example, stems, leaves, roots, arms, wings, legs).

FIRST GRADE: EARTH SCIENCES STANDARD 3

Weather can be observed, measured, and described. As a basis for understanding these concepts:

✓ Students know how to use simple tools (such as a thermometer or wind vane) to measure weather conditions and record changes from day to day and across the seasons.

✓ Students know that the weather changes from day to day but that trends in temperature of rain (or snow) tend to be predictable during a season.

✓ Students know the sun warms the land, air, and water.

THIRD GRADE: LIFE SCIENCES STANDARD 3

Adaptations in physical structure or behavior may improve an organism's chance for survival. As a basis for understanding this concept:

✓ Students know plants and animals have structures that serve different functions in growth, survival, and reproduction.

✓ Students know examples of diverse life forms in different environments, such as oceans, deserts, tundra, forests, grasslands, and wetlands.

✓ Students know living things cause changes in the environment in which they live; some of these changes are detrimental to the organism or other organisms, and some are beneficial.

✓ Students know when the environment changes, some plants and animals survive and reproduce; others die or move to new locations.

✓ Students know that some kinds of organisms that once lived on Earth have completely disappeared.

Signs, pots, and seedling trays.

RESOURCES

Innumerable resources are available on the subjects of school gardens, outdoor classrooms, green schoolyards, and environmental education. A little research into the history of the movement and the support organizations that exist will help you in your process. While we have listed many subject areas and relevant resources here, this is just a sample of what is available to help get you started in your research. The bibliography also has extensive resources for further reading.

SCHOOL GARDEN–RELATED ORGANIZATIONS

Many organizations around the globe either directly or indirectly support school gardens and green schoolyards. We have been fortunate to work with several of the organizations listed here. Each has plentiful online information, resources, and links for you to delve into.

Boston Schoolyard Initiative
Boston, Massachusetts
www.schoolyards.org
The goal of the Boston Schoolyard Initiative (BSI) is to design and build multi-use open spaces that complement the primary mission of the school: to preserve and foster children's innate sense of curiosity and give them the tools and skills needed to become lifelong learners. The BSI helps in-school and out-of-school teachers work with students to design and build schoolyards that provide a rich environment for teaching and learning. BSI has developed a supplement to the FOSS (Full Option Science System) kit curriculum for teaching lessons in an outdoor classroom.

California School Garden Network
www.csgn.org
The California School Garden Network is a research-based organization founded to created and sustain school gardens in every school in California. This Web site is an invaluable resource for grant information as well as for garden-based learning research.

Center for Ecoliteracy
Berkeley, California
www.ecoliteracy.org
The Center for Ecoliteracy is dedicated to education for sustainable living.

City Farmer
Vancouver, British Columbia
www.cityfarmer.org
www.cityfarmer.info
City Farmer is Canada's Office of Urban Agriculture. Their Web sites, cityfarmer.org and cityfarmer.info, host "Urban Agriculture Notes" and provide information and links on urban agriculture. City Farmer's mission is to teach people how to grow food in the city, compost their waste, and take care of their home landscape in an environmentally responsible way.

Cornell Garden-Based Learning Program
Department of Horticulture
Ithaca, New York
blogs.cornell.edu/garden/
www.hort.cornell.edu/gbl/index.html
The Cornell Garden-Based Learning Program encompasses activities and projects in which the garden is the foundation for integrated learning and discovery across disciplines, through active, engaging real-world experiences that are relevant to children, youth, adults, and communities.

Cultivating Community
Portland, Maine
www.cultivatingcommunity.org
Cultivating Community is a nonprofit organization that uses organic, sustainable practices to grow food in community and school gardens as well as at partnering farms and to distribute to those in need. Their community food work serves as an engine for high-impact youth and community development programs that reconnect people to the natural and social systems that sustain us all.

EcoSchool Design
Berkeley, California
www.ecoschools.com/index.html
Ecological schoolyards are outdoor learning environments that teach ecological principles through the design of the schoolyard landscape. They can substantially improve the appearance of school grounds while creating hands-on resources that allow teachers to lead exciting "field trips" without ever leaving school property. EcoSchool Design seeks to assist schools, and those who care about them, in transforming paved schoolyards into vibrant ecosystems for outdoor learning. The Web site, run by Bay Tree Design, Inc., is an information hub for green schoolyards.

Edible Schoolyard (Berkeley)
Berkeley, California
www.edibleschoolyard.org
The Edible Schoolyard, established in 1995, is a one-acre garden and kitchen classroom at Martin Luther King, Jr. Middle School in Berkeley, California. It is a program of the Chez Panisse Foundation, a nonprofit organization founded by chef and author Alice Waters.

Edible Schoolyard (New Orleans)
New Orleans, Louisiana
www.esynola.org
The mission of Edible Schoolyard New Orleans is to create and sustain an expansive organic garden on the public school campus of Samuel J. Green Charter School in New Orleans.

Evergreen Toyota Learning Grounds, Canada
Toronto, Ontario
www.evergreen.ca
Evergreen Toyota's Learning Grounds program motivates and supports schools in bringing nature to their school grounds. Creating outdoor classrooms provides students with a healthy and safe place to play, as well as learn and develop a genuine respect for nature and each other. The Evergreen Learning Grounds Web site has an extensive library of resources for starting and sustaining green schoolyards and outdoor classrooms.

Growing Schools Garden
London, UK
www.thegrowingschoolsgarden.org.uk
The Growing Schools Garden encourages teachers to use the outdoor classroom as a resource across the curriculum for pupils of all ages and abilities.

Garden Organic
Warwickshire, UK
www.gardenorganic.org.uk
Garden Organic, a UK national charity for organic growing, has a Web site dedicated to primary and secondary schools containing regularly updated advice on what to do in the school garden.

Junior Master Gardener Program (JMG)
Ventura, California
www.jmgkids.com
JMG's mission is to grow good kids by igniting a passion for learning, success and service through a unique gardening education.

Life Lab Science Program
Santa Cruz, California
www.lifelab.org
Life Lab offers curriculum and professional development for educators implementing garden-based learning programs. Life Lab coordi-

nates staff development efforts throughout California and at the Life Lab Garden Classroom, located at the University of California, Santa Cruz. The two-acre Life Lab Garden Classroom is a model outdoor learning center offering school field trips as well as after-school and community programs.

National Agriculture in the Classroom (NAIC)
Washington, DC
www.agclassroom.org
NAIC is a grassroots program coordinated by the United States Department of Agriculture. Its goal is to help students gain a greater awareness of the role of agriculture in the economy and society so that they may become citizens who support wise agricultural policies.

National Gardening Association
South Burlington, Vermont
www.kidsgardening.com
Kidsgardening.com, an online resource devoted to gardening with children, hosted on the National Gardening Association's Web site, has a full range of resources available, including: planting ideas, curriculum suggestions, and online links. The National Gardening Association also has a well-stocked online store that specializes in products related to gardening with children, including child-sized hand tools.

Occidental Arts and Ecology Center (OAEC)
Occidental, California
www.oaec.org
OAEC offers a five-day intensive residential training program for creating and developing school gardens. The program covers such topics as curricula linked to state standards, hands-on gardening, nutrition, cooking from the garden, team building, grants, fundraising, recycling, project-based learning, and touring school sites.

Real School Gardens
Fort Worth, Texas
www.realschoolgardens.org
Real School Gardens cultivates relationships with elementary school communities to create learning gardens that raise hope, spark imaginations, and connect children to nature.

Making a nest. *Photo by Brooke Hieserich*

San Francisco Green Schoolyard Alliance (SFGSA)
San Francisco, California
www.sfgreenschools.org
The SFGSA supports existing school gardens as well as schoolyard transformations from ordinary asphalt yards into ecologically rich green spaces for learning and play. The SFGSA works to ensure that these emerging vibrant landscapes reflect their site's local ecology along with their school community's green schoolyard goals and curricula. The SFGSA can help schools find a wide variety of resources to improve their schoolyards.

Learning through Landscapes
www.ltl.org.uk
Learning through Landscapes is a UK-based organization that helps schools and other early education environments make the most of their outdoor spaces for play and learning.

COMPOSTING/VERMICOMPOSTING

California Integrated Waste Management Board
www.ciwmb.ca.gov/organics/worms/

Environmental Protection Agency (EPA)
www.epa.gov/osw/conserve/rrr/composting/vermi.htm

Food to Flowers!
San Francisco, California
www.sfenvironment.org
SF Environment's Food to Flowers program turns lunchroom waste into nutrient-rich compost and features schoolwide assemblies that teach about the interconnectedness of nature and how recycling and composting protect the environment.

New Mexico State
http://aces.nmsu.edu/pubs/_h/h-164.pdf

The Rodale Institute
www.rodaleinstitute.org
Rodale Institute is a nonprofit that creates global solutions from the ground up. Founded in Kutztown, Pennsylvania, in 1947 by organic pioneer J. I. Rodale, they publish *Organic Gardening* magazine and a composting handbook, *The Rodale Book of Composting*.

CURRICULUM AND TRAINING

Closing the Loop: Exploring Integrated Waste Management and Resource Conservation
Sacramento, California
www.ciwmb.ca.gov/Schools/Curriculum/CTL/
Closing the Loop is a compilation of fifty lessons to help students discover and nurture an environmental ethic and stewardship for natural resources. The activities focus on solid waste and environmental awareness topics including landfills, recycling, packaging, resource conservation, waste prevention, worm composting, and more. Each lesson encourages students to explore their natural environment, identify waste management issues, and engage in personal and community action projects.

Earth Steward Gardener Curriculum
Portland, Maine
www.cultivatingcommunity.org
The Earth Steward Gardener Curriculum, produced by Cultivating Community in Portland, Maine, provides seasonal garden and food activities that help kids understand how we're all connected to the land, our communities, and each other.

Foss Science (Full Option Science System)
Berkeley, California
www.fossweb.com
FOSS is a research-based science curriculum for grades K–8 developed at the Lawrence Hall of Science, University of California at Berkeley.

Garden Mosaics
Ithaca, New York
www.gardenmosaics.org
Garden Mosaics is a science education program that combines intergenerational mentoring, community action, and understanding different cultures at the Department of Natural Resources, Cornell University.

Great Explorations in Math and Science (GEMS)
Berkeley, California
www.lhsgems.org
Developed at the Lawrence Hall of Science, UC Berkeley, GEMS publishes science and math curricula, offers professional development, and maintains an international support network.

Growing Communities Curriculum
Columbus, Ohio
www.communitygarden.org
The Growing Communities Curriculum, produced by the American Community Gardening Association (ACGA), provides an in-depth exploration of the practices and strategies community organizers can use to develop dynamic leaders and create strong programs using a participatory approach to community building.

Life Lab Science Program
Santa Cruz, California
www.lifelab.org
See description under School Garden–Related Organizations.

Math in the Garden
Berkeley, California
http://botanicalgarden.berkeley.edu/education/eduMIG.shtml
Math in the Garden, developed by the University of California Botanical Garden in Berkeley, uses a mathematical lens to explore the magical arena of gardens. Colorful watercolor illustrations depict children, youth, and adults discovering patterns, measuring crops, tasting new fruits and vegetables, planting in circles, and graphing their observations of fruits, flowers, and shadows. The University of California Botanical Garden, in collaboration with the Lawrence Hall of Science, has developed engaging math activities that anyone can do.

National Environmental Education Week School Garden Curricula
http://eeweek.org/resources/garden_curricula.htm#5-8
National Environmental Education Week (EE Week) is the largest organized environmental education event in the United States. EE Week increases the educational impact of Earth Day by creating a full week of educational preparation, learning, and activities in K–12 classrooms, nature centers, zoos, museums, and aquariums.

ENVIRONMENTAL EDUCATION RESOURCES AND ORGANIZATIONS

Calgary Zoo: Grounds for Change Schoolyard Naturalization Program
Calgary, Alberta, Canada
www.calgaryzoo.org/schoolyard_naturalization/
Schools in Calgary began naturalizing their schoolyards in the mid-1990s, and the Calgary Zoo has been a leader in the movement since 1998. The Grounds for Change program is designed as a resource to offer the experiences of more than forty Calgary-area schools. It provides insight into successful methods for planning and maintaining school sites and how to use the naturalized areas to complement classroom teaching.

The Centre for Alternative Technology
Powys (Wales), UK
www.cat.org.uk
The Centre for Alternative Technology offers solutions to issues such as climate change, pollution and the waste of precious resources.

Council for Environmental Education (CEE)
Houston, Texas
www.councilforee.org/
www.projectwild.org/
www.wetcity.org/
www.flyingwild.org/
For more than thirty-five years, CEE has provided environmental education programs and services that promote stewardship of the environment and further the capacity of learners to make informed decisions. CEE's programs include: Project WILD, Flying WILD, and WET in the City.

Ecology Center of Berkeley
Berkeley, California
www.ecologycenter.org
The Ecology Center's environmental resource center provides information and tools for eco-friendly living. Their library contains many books, videos, and periodicals including curriculum guides and lesson plans, gardening and children's books, and other resources.

The Great Plant Hunt
London, UK
www.greatplanthunt.org/
To mark the 200th anniversary of Charles Darwin's birth, the Royal Botanic Gardens, Kew, commissioned and funded by the Wellcome Trust, has created The Great Plant Hunt. This exciting project encourages children to explore the natural world around them and join other schools in the biggest ever school science project. Forming part of the Darwin 200 initiative, The Great Plant Hunt invites primary school children to follow in the footsteps of Darwin by going on nature walks in and around their school grounds. They'll find out more about plants and in the process learn key scientific skills.

North American Association for Environmental Education (NAAEE)
Washington, DC
www.naaee.org
NAAEE is the professional association for environmental education. Members promote professional excellence in nonformal organizations, K–12 classrooms, universities (both instructors and students), government agencies, and corporate settings throughout North America and in more than fifty-five other countries.

The Pollinator Partnership
San Francisco, California
www.pollinator.org
The Pollinator Partnership works to protect the health of managed and native pollinating animals vital to North American ecosystems and agriculture. Their Web site is a source of information for consumers, gardeners, land managers, educators, resource managers, producers, and farmers to help pollinators, essential components for all of life.

Project WET
Bozeman, Montana
http://projectwet.org/
Since 1984, Project WET has dedicated itself to the mission of reaching children, parents, teachers, and community members of the world with water education.

Discovery in the school garden can be simple.

A row of container beds.

The Trust for Public Land (TPL):
Bay Area Parks for People Program
San Francisco, California
www.tpl.org
The mission of TPL's Parks for People Program is to create quality public spaces that revitalize low-income communities and link them to nature, history, and place. The program strives to reach a balance between connecting residents to nature and providing opportunities for active recreation.

The Watershed Project
Richmond, California
www.thewatershedproject.org
The Watershed Project is an environmental education nonprofit. Their mission is to educate and inspire communities to protect their local watershed. The Watershed Project offers a number of workshops for those interested in school gardening, including an introduction to school gardening, a school garden design course, and a cooking and nutrition course.

FARM TO SCHOOL

National Farm to School
www.farmtoschool.org
Farm to School brings healthy food from local farms to school children nationwide. The program teaches students about the path from farm to fork, and instills healthy eating habits that can last a lifetime. At the same time, use of local produce in school meals and educational activities provides a new direct market for farmers in the area and mitigates environmental impacts of transporting food long distances.

FILMS

These films about agriculture and nutrition could be useful as educational tools.

Food Inc.
www.foodincmovie.com

Nourish Life
www.nourishlife.org

Cob is a mixture of sand, clay, and straw.

Videos by permaculture founder, Bill Mollison
www.bullfrogfilms.com/catalog/tgghv.html

The Real Dirt on Farmer John
www.pbs.org/independentlens/realdirt

The True Cost of Food
www.sierraclub.org/truecostoffood

GRANT-MAKING ORGANIZATIONS

Some of these organizations are described further elsewhere in this list of resources. Grant opportunities are often located under a "resources" or "grants" tab on their Web sites.

California School Garden Network
www.csgn.org
See description under School Garden–Related Organizations.

Donor's Choose
Washington, DC
www.donorschoose.org
An online charity that connects donors to particular classroom projects.

National Gardening Association
www.kidsgardening.org
See description under School Garden–Related Organizations.

National Fish and Wildlife Foundation
www.nfwf.org
The National Fish and Wildlife Foundation (NFWF) is a non-profit organization that preserves and restores our nation's native wildlife species and habitats. Created by Congress in 1984, NFWF directs public conservation dollars to the most pressing environmental needs and matches those investments with private funds.

The Foundation Center
www.foundationcenter.org
Established in 1956 and currently supported by close to 550 foundations, the Foundation Center is an excellent resource for locating funding opportunities.

PEST INFORMATION AND NATURAL PEST CONTROL

Be sure to check your local cooperative extension for more pest control information.

National Gardening Association: Pest Control Library
www.garden.org/pestlibrary
The National Garden Association maintains an extensive pest control library on their Web site, covering topics on insect and animal pests as well as plant diseases.

SEED SUPPLIERS

Botanical Interests
Broomfield, Colorado
www.botanicalinterests.com

Fedco Seeds
Waterville, Maine
www.fedcoseeds.com

Johnny's Selected Seeds
Winslow, Maine
www.johnnyseeds.com

Renee's Garden Seeds
Felton, California
www.reneesgarden.com

Seeds of Change
Santa Fe, New Mexico
www.seedsofchange.com

Seed Savers Exchange
www.seedsavers.org

The Non-GMO Sourcebook
www.non-gmoreport.com

A schoolyard mosaic. *Design by Paul Lanier and Nancy Thompson*

SOIL TESTING

Check your local nursery or hardware store for basic soil test kits if you only need a general idea of the nutrient content of your soil and its pH. If you need a more in-depth test of your soil, particularly for contaminants, refer to the listings here.

A & L Western Laboratories
Modesto, California
www.al-labs-west.com
This laboratory can test soil, plants, and water for metals and pesticides. Check their Web site or call for instructions on collecting soil samples and to obtain a soil test form and rate sheet with prices for a variety of different tests.

Farmers Weekly Agricultural Register
www.agregister.co.uk

Soil Foodweb Oregon
Corvallis, Oregon
www.oregonfoodweb.com
www.soilfoodweb.com
This lab provides information on the living organisms in your soil, rather than focusing on the mineral content and type of soil.

Soil & Plant Tissue Testing Laboratory,
University of Massachusetts
Amherst, Massachusetts
www.umass.edu/plsoils/soiltest
The University of Massachusetts provides one of the least expensive standard soil tests, and also has a variety of other soil tests including tests for metals (lead, cadmium, chromium, and nickel).

SOLAR ENERGY

The Solar Schoolhouse
Martinez, California
www.solarschoolhouse.org
The Solar School house is a K–12 energy program that uses the sun as a starting point for teaching about energy resources, conservation, and other energy topics.

Breathing Places, Royal Society for the Protection of Birds
www.rspb.org.uk

With the help of BBC Breathing Places Schools, nature can be nurtured and encouraged in schools for children to enjoy and explore. More than 10,000 schools across the UK have registered to take part in BBC Breathing Places Schools. Each term, schools are asked to "Do One Thing" for nature. Activities include seed planting, feeding wildlife, and creating wildlife homes and water habitats.

National Wildlife Federation: Schoolyard Habitats Program
www.nwf.org

The Schoolyard Habitats Program assists school communities in the use of school grounds as learning sites for wildlife conservation and cross-curricular learning. Through the Schoolyard Habitats certification program, the National Wildlife Federation (NWF) recognizes the accomplishments of, and fosters networking among, innovative school communities nationwide. This K–12 program provides opportunities to create, build and maintain living classrooms and is an exceptional way for students, teachers and community members to work together.

The Wildlife Trusts
Nottinghamshire, UK
www.wildlifetrusts.org

The Wildlife Trusts is a voluntary organization dedicated to conversing the full range of the UK's habitats and species. Its goals are to stand up for wildlife and the environment, to create and enhance wildlife havens, to inspire people about the natural world, and to foster sustainable living.

BIBLIOGRAPHY

Applehof, Mary. 1997. *Worms Eat My Garbage: How to Set Up and Maintain a Worm Composting System*. Kalamazoo, MI: Flower Press.

Banana Slug String Band. 1989. *Dirt Made My Lunch*. Compact disc. Available at www.bananaslugstringband.com.

Bloomfield, Jill. 2008. *Grow It, Cook It: Simple Gardening Projects and Delicious Recipes*. London: DK Publishing.

Brennan, Georgeanne and Ethel Brennan. 2004. *The Children's Kitchen Garden: A Book of Gardening, Cooking, and Learning*. Berkeley, CA: Ten Speed Press.

Broda, Herbert. 2007. *Schoolyard Enhanced Learning: Using the Outdoors as an Instructional Tool, K–8*. Portland, ME: Stenhouse.

Burdette, Hillary L., and Robert C. Whitaker. 2005. *Resurrecting Free Play in Young Children: Looking Beyond Fitness and Fatness to Attention, Affiliation, and Affect*. Chicago: American Medical Association.

California School Garden Network. 2006. Gardens for Learning: Creating and Sustaining Your School Garden. www.csgn.org/page.php?id=36

Canadian Council on Learning. 2006. Let the children play: Nature's answer to learning. Early Childhood Learning Knowledge Centre. www.ccl-cca.ca/CCL/Reports/LessonsInLearning/LinL20061010LearninPlay.htm

Center for Ecoliteracy. 1997. Getting Started: A Guide for Creating School Gardens as Outdoor Classrooms. www.ecoliteracy.org/publications/getting-started.html

Clements, R. 2004. An investigation of the state of outdoor play. *Contemporary Issues in Early Childhood* 5 (1): 68–80.

Coleman, Eliot. 2009. *The Winter Harvest Handbook: Year-Round Vegetable Production Using Deep Organic Techniques and Unheated Greenhouses*. White River Junction, VT: Chelsea Green.

Cornell, Joseph. 1998. *Sharing Nature with Children*. Nevada City, CA: Dawn Publications.

Danks, Sharon. 2010. *Asphalt to Ecosystems: Design Ideas for Schoolyard Transformations*. Oakland, CA: New Village Press.

Dannenmaier, Molly. 2008. *A Child's Garden: 60 Ideas to Make Any Garden Come Alive for Children*. Portland, OR: Timber Press.

Denzer, Kiko. 2007. *Build Your Own Earth Oven*. Blodgett, OR: Hand Print Press.

Desmond, D., J. Grieshop, and A. Subramaniam. 2003. Revisiting garden-based learning in basic education: Philosophical roots, historical foundations, best practices and products, impacts, outcomes, and future directions. Food and Agriculture Organization of the United Nations (FAO). www.fao.org/sd/2003/kn0504_en.htm

Gershuny, Grace, and Deborah L. Martin, eds. 1992. *The Rodale Book of Composting*. Emmaus, PA: Rodale Books.

Grant, Tim, and Gail Littlejohn, eds. 2001. Greening school grounds: Creating habitats for learning. In *Green Teacher*. Gabriola Island, BC: New Society Publishing.

Gross, Phyllis, and Esther P. Railton 1972. *Teaching Science in an Outdoor Environment* Berkeley, CA: University of California Press.

Harmonious Technologies. 1995. *Backyard Composting*. Ojai, CA: Harmonious Technologies.

Herd, Meg. 1997. *Learn and Play in the Garden: Games, Crafts and Activities for Children*. Hauppauge, NY: Barron's.

Hinchman, Hannah. 1997. *A Trail Through Leaves: The Journals as a Path to Place*. New York: Norton.

Jeavons, Jon. 2006. *How to Grow More Vegetables: (and Fruits, Nuts, Berries, Grains, and Other Crops) Than You Ever Thought Possible on Less Land Than You Can Imagine*. Berkeley, CA: Ten Speed Press.

Karsten, L. 2005. It all used to be better? Different generations on continuity and change in urban children's daily use of space. *Children's Geographies* 3 (3): 275–290.

Katzen, Molly. 2004. *Pretend Soup and Other Real Recipes: A Cookbook for Preschoolers and Up*. Berkeley, CA: Tricycle Press.

Keator, Glenn. 1990. *Complete Garden Guide to the Native Plants of California*. San Francisco: Chronicle Books.

Keifer, Joseph, and Martin Kemple. 1998. *Digging Deeper: Integrating Youth Gardens into Schools and Communities*. Food Works.

Kellert, Stephen R. 2005. Nature and childhood development. In *Building for Life: Designing and Understanding the Human-Nature Connection*. Washington, DC: Island Press.

Klemmer, C. D., T. M. Waliczek, and J. M. Zajicek. 2005. Growing minds: The effect of a school gardening program on the science achievement of elementary students. *HortTechnology* 15 (3): 448–452.

Kraus, Sibella. 2002. *Kids Cook Farm Fresh Foods: Seasonal Recipes, Activities, and Farm Profiles that Teach Ecological Responsibility*. Sacramento, CA: California Dept. of Education Press.

Lanza, Patricia. 1998. *Lasagna Gardening: A New Layering System for Bountiful Gardens*. Emmaus, PA: Rodale.

Libman, K. 2007. Growing youth growing food: How vegetable gardening influences young people's food consciousness and eating habits. *Applied Environmental Education & Communication* 6 (1): 87–95.

Lieberman, Gerald A., and Linda L. Hoody. 1998. *Closing the Achievement Gap: Using the Environment as an Integrating Context for Learning*. Poway, CA: State Education and Environment Roundtable.

Liebreich, Karen, Jutta Wagner, and Annette Wendland. 2009. *The Family Kitchen Garden*. Portland, OR: Timber Press.

Lineberger, S. E., and J. M. Zajicek,. 2000. School gardens: Can a hands-on teaching tool affect students' attitudes and behaviors regarding fruit and vegetables? *Hort-Technology* 10 (3): 593–597.

Lingelback, Jenepher, and Lisa Purcel. 2000. *Hands on Nature, Information and Activities for Exploring the Environment with Children, Vermont Institute of Natural Science.* Woodstock, VT: Vermont Institute of Natural Science.

Louv, Richard. 2008. *Last Child in the Woods: Saving our Children from Nature-Deficit Disorder.* Chapel Hill: Algonquin Books.

Lovejoy, Sharon. 1999. *Roots, Shoots, Buckets, & Boots.* New York: Workman Publishing Company.

Lovejoy, Sharon. 2001. *Sunflower Houses: A Book for Children and Their Grown-Ups.* New York: Workman.

Margolin, Malcolm. 1981. *The Ohlone Way.* Berkeley, CA: Heyday Books.

Mayer-Smith, J., O. Bartosh, and L. Peterat. 2007. Teaming children and elders to grow food and environmental consciousness. *Applied Environmental Education & Communication* 6 (1): 77–85.

McAleese, J. D., and L. L. Rankin. 2007. Garden-based nutrition education affects fruit and vegetable consumption in six grade adolescents. *Journal of the American Dietetic Association* 107: 662–665.

Morris, J., and S. Zidenberg-Cherr. 2002. Garden-enhanced nutrition curriculum improves fourth-grade school children's knowledge of nutrition and preference for vegetables. *Journal of the American Dietetic Association* 102 (1), 91–93.

Ogden, C. L., M. D. Carroll, L. R. Curtin, M. A. McDowell, C. J. Tabak, and K. M. Flegal. 2006. Prevalence of overweight and obesity in the United States, 1999–2004. *Journal of the American Medical Association* 295 (13): 1549–1555.

Patten, Elizabeth. 2003. *Healthy Foods from Healthy Soils: A Hands-On Resource for Teachers.* Gardiner, ME: Tilbury House.

Payne, Binet. 1999. *The Worm Café: Mid-Scale Composting of Lunchroom Wastes.* Kalamazoo, MI: Flower Press.

Pierce, Pam. 2002. *Golden Gate Gardening: Year-Round Food Gardening in the San Francisco Bay Area and Coastal California.* Seattle: Sasquatch Books.

Pollan, Michael. 2001. *The Botany of Desire: A Plant's-Eye View of the World.* New York: Random House.

Pollan, Michael. 2007. *Omnivore's Dilemma: A Natural History of Four Meals.* New York: Penguin Books.

Pollan, Michael. 2009. *In Defense of Food: An Eater's Manifesto.* New York: Penguin Books.

Pranis, Eve. 1992. *GrowLab Curriculum Study.* Burlington, VT: National Gardening Association.

Pranis, Eve. 2008. *Nourishing Choices: Implementing Food Education in classrooms, Cafeterias, and Schoolyards.* National Gardening Association. South Burlington, VT: National Gardening Association.

Rhoades, Dianne. 1995. *Garden Crafts for Kids: Fifty Great Reasons to Get Your Hands Dirty.* New York: Sterling Publishing.

Rideout, V., and E. Hamel. 2006. *The Media Family: Electronic Media in the Lives of Infants, Toddlers, Preschoolers, and Their Parents.* Washington, DC: Kaiser Family Foundation.

Rivkin, Mary S. 1995. *The Great Outdoors, Restoring Children's Right to Play Outside* Washington, DC: National Association for the Education of Young Children.

Roberts, D. F., U. Foehr, and V. Rideout. 2005. *Generation M: Media in the Lives of 8 to 18 Year Olds*. Washington, DC: Kaiser Family Foundation.

Robinson, Carolyn W., and J. M. Zajicek. 2005. Growing minds: The effects of a one-year school garden program on six constructs of life skills of elementary school children. *HortTechnology* 15 (3): 453–457.

Sibley, David Allen. 2000. *Sibley Guide to Birds*. New York: Knopf.

Skelly, S. M., and J. M. Zajicek. 1998. The effect of an interdisciplinary garden program on the environmental attitudes of elementary school students. *HortTechnology* 8 (4): 579–583.

Sobel, David. 2004. *Place-Based Education: Connecting Classrooms and Communities* Great Barrington, MA: The Orion Society.

State Education and Environment Roundtable (SEER). 2000. *California Student Assessment Project*. Poway, CA: California Department of Education.

State Education and Environment Roundtable (SEER). 2005. *California Student Assessment Project Phase Two: The Effects of Environment-Based Education on Student Achievement*. Poway, CA: California Department of Education.

Toyota Evergreen Learning Grounds. 2000. *All Hands in the Dirt*. Toronto: Evergreen.

Trelstad, B. 1997. Little Machines in their gardens: A history of school gardens in America, 1891–1920. *Landscape Journal* 16 (2): 161–173.

Troiano, R. P., K. M. Flegal, R. J. Kuczmarski, S. M. Campbell, and C. L. Johnson. 1995. Overweight prevalence and trends for children and adolescents: The national-health and nutrition examination surveys, 1963 to 1991. *Archives of Pediatrics and Adolescent Medicine* 149 (10): 1085–1091.

Warnes, Jon. 2001. Living Willow Sculpture. Kent, UK: Search Press.

Waters, Marjorie. 1994. *Victory Garden Kids' Book*. New York: Globe Pequot.

Wridt, Pamela J. 2004. An historical analysis of young people's use of public space, parks and playgrounds in New York city. *Children, Youth, and Environments* 14 (1): 86–106.

CHILDREN'S BOOKS

Aliki. 1986. *Corn Is Maize: The Gift of the Indians.* New York: HarperCollins.

Anthony, Joseph. 1997. *The Dandelion Seed.* Nevada City, CA: Dawn Publications.

Aston, Diana Hutts. 2007. *A Seed Is Sleepy.* San Francisco: Chronicle Books.

Azarian, Mary. 2000. *A Gardener's Alphabet.* Boston: Houghton Mifflin Publishers.

Barner, Bob. *1999. Bugs! Bugs! Bugs!* San Francisco: Chronicle Books.

Brown, Ruth. 2001. *Ten Seeds.* New York: Knopf.

Doyle, Malachy. 2002. *Jody's Beans.* Boston: Candlewick.

Ehlert, Lois. 1988. *Planting a Rainbow.* New York: Harcourt Brace Jovanovich.

Fleischman, Paul. 2002. *Weslandia.* Cambridge, MA: Candlewick.

Fleischman, Paul. 2004. *Seed Folks.* New York: HarperTeen.

French, Vivian. 1995. *Oliver's Vegetables.* New York: Orchard.

Greenstein, Elaine. 2004. *One Little Seed.* New York: Viking.

Havill, Juanita. 2006. *I Heard It from Alice Zucchini: Poems about the Garden.* San Francisco: Chronicle Books.

Krauss, Ruth. 2005. *The Carrot Seed.* New York: HarperCollins.

McMillan, Bruce. 1991. *Eating Fractions.* New York: Scholastic Press.

Nagro, Anne. 2008. *Our Generous Garden.* Wilmette, IL: Dancing Rhinoceros Press.

Roberts, Bethany. 2001. *The Wind's Garden.* New York: Henry Holt.

Roemer, Heidi Bee. 2006. *What Kinds of Seeds Are These?* Minnetonka, MN: NorthWord.

Rosen, Michael J. 1998. *Down to Earth.* New York: Harcourt.

WEB SITES

American Botanical Society
www.herbalgram.org

American Horticultural Society
www.ahs.org

Bay Tree Design, Inc. /EcoSchool Design
www.ecoschools.com

Butterflies and Moths of North America
www.butterfliesandmoths.org/map

California Foundation for Agriculture in the Classroom
www.cfaitc.org

Center for Agroecology and Sustainable Food Systems
http://casfs.ucsc.edu/

Container Gardening: University of Illinois Extension
http://urbanext.illinois.edu/containergardening/default.cfm

Cubic yard calculator
www.nationalmulch.com/underco.htm

DC Schoolyard Greening
www.dcschoolyardgreening.org/

Garden ABCs
www.gardenabcs.com/

Garden in Every School, California Department
of Education
www.cde.ca.gov/Ls/nu/he/garden.asp

How to Compost
www.howtocompost.org

Life Cycles Project, Canada
http://lifecyclesproject.ca/

Organic Gardening
www.organicgardening.com

Outdoor Biology Instructional Strategies (OBIS)
www.outdoorinquiry.com

Rebuilding Together
www.rebuildingtogether.org/
This group is a good contact for construction help
at your school.

Roots to Health
www.rootstohealth.org/

Rose Hayden-Smith, University of California
Hayden-Smith is an expert in the history of
school gardens.
http://ceventura.ucdavis.edu/sbdisplay/stafflist.
    cfm?county=2372
http://ucanr.org/seek/anrdirectoryinfo.
    cfm?index=958
www.foodandsocietyfellows.org/about/fellow/
    rose-hayden-smith

Sustainable Agriculture Education (SAGE)
www.sagecenter.org

School Garden Weekly
http://schoolgardenweekly.com/

School Garden Wizard
www.schoolgardenewizard.org

Shelburne Farms
www.shelburnefarms.org

Urban Nutrition Initiative, Philadelphia, PA
www.urbannutrition.org/index.html

INDEX

A

administrative support, 38
Alice Fong Yu Alternative
    School, 171
alliums, 138
amendments, soil, 105, 106, 108
Americans with Disabilities
    Act, 23, 177, 181
annual fund, 45, 46
anti-fungal spray, 114
art in the garden, 97, 121
arugula (rocket), 132, 139, 141
asphalt, removal of, 52, 109
at-will crops, 144

B

back-to-school night, 130
basic garden tasks, 119
Basic Stir Fry, 188
beans, 132, 139, 141
beekeepers, 100, 102
beets, 132, 135, 141
bender board, 65
beneficial insects, 115
benefits of school gardens, 26
bok choi, 141
borage, 133
broadcast seeding, 136
broccoli, 132, 139
brussels sprouts, 132, 139
budgeting, 72, 76, 79, 80
bunching onions, 132, 141

C

calendula, 133
carrots, 132, 139, 141
cauliflower, 132, 139
chard, 132, 139, 141
cherry tomatoes, 141
chives, 141
cistern. *See* rainwater harvesting
classroom management, 94, 122
cold house. *See* hoop house
cole crops, 132
Coleman, Eliot, 156
collards, 132, 139, 141
community and social develop-
    ment, 32, 82
community-building, 83, 128
community service, 97
community work days, 128
compost, 106
compost tea, 113
container gardening, 66, 67
content standards, 89, 195
cooking in the garden, 131, 147
cooking supplies, 121, 146, 185
copper tape, 115
coriander, 133
cover crops, 106
cucumber, 133, 139
curriculum, 79. *See also* garden-
    based curricula
custodial staff, 127
cut and come again, 141

D

digging area, 95
dill, 133
direct seeding versus seedlings,
    135, 139
dishwashing, 145
dividing a class, 95, 124
donations, 130
drainage, 52, 59, 111
drawings, 59
dry-erase board, 53, 60, 63

E

earthworms, 105
Edible Flower Canapés, 191
elements of a school garden, 52
environmental stewardship
    ethic, 32
equipment, 129
evaluations, 100, 101

F

fencing, 57
fertilizers, 106, 108, 113
field trips, 99
fish emulsion, 113
food systems garden, 131
foundations. *See* fundraising
free play, 34
Fresh Apples and Local
    Cheeses, 194

Fresh Pea, Pumpkin Seed, and Garlic Dip, 189
fruit trees, 52, 166, 187
fundraising, 73, 81–84

G

garden-based curricula, 89, 90, 91. *See also* curriculum
garden committee, 129
garden coordinator, 87, 89
garden design, 47, 48
garden library, 79
garden party, 130
garden plan, 59
Garden Scavenger Hunt, 166
garden schedule, 118
garlic, 132, 139, 141
gathering area, 53
goals of a school garden, 43
gophers, 92
grant writing. *See* fundraising
Graphing Plant Growth, 163
greenhouse, 134
groundbreaking, 72–76

H

Habitat Riddles, 158
habitats, 153
hands-on learning, 15, 29
harvesting, 140
healthy outdoor classroom, 103
Herb and Edible Flower Salad, 186
history of school gardens, 18
Honey Lemon Sauté, 188
hoop house, 156
hose bibbs, 57
hygiene, 140, 145

I

identifying garden users, 46
imaginative play, 34
in-ground planting, 67
initial expenses, 72
in-kind support, 59, 73
insecticidal soap, 114
insects, 91, 105, 114, 115, 121
Interviewing Local Farmers, 165
Introduction to Worm Composting, An, 160
irrigation, 57, 125

J

journaling, 92

K

kale, 132
kitchen tools, 185

L

landscape architects, 59, 60
Land Scarcity, 163
lasagna gardening, 112
leeks, 132, 139, 141
Lemon Olive Oil Dressing, 187
Lemon Verbena Raspberry Sorbet, 193
lesson plans, 90, 118
lettuce, 132, 135, 139, 141
life skills, 136
listservs, 42
livestock troughs, 66, 67
local movement, 180
Look Lively, 153
Louv, Richard, 24

M

maintenance plan, 127
maintenance tips, 125

manure, 108
microorganisms, 105
mint, 133
mortar and pestle, 146
mosaics, 121
mulching, 105, 109

N

nasturtium, 133
native plants, 58
natural phenomena, 90
nature play, 34
nitrogen, 106
No Child Left Inside Act, 24
no-till gardening. *See* lasagna gardening
nutrition education, 29, 30, 131

O

obesity, 23, 29, 30
onions, 132, 139, 141
oregano, 133
organic gardening, 105, 113
outdoor classroom, 39, 53, 60

P

parent associations, 46
parsley, 133
Pasta with Garlicky Greens, 192
pathways, 53, 64
peas, 132, 139, 141
peppers, 133, 139
pesticides, 103
pests, 103
pickup truck, 128
planter boxes, 62, 63
planting, 133
planting beds, 62
planting times, 132
plastic lumber, 65
Pollution Soup, 167

portable seating, 53, 62
potatoes, 139, 143
Preserving the Legacy, 151
pressure-treated wood, 65
professional development, 79, 99
programmatic tips, 118
publicity, 96

R
radishes, 132, 135, 144
rainmakers, 125
rainwater harvesting, 52
raised beds, 62, 63
recipes, 185
record keeping, 76, 90, 118, 119
recycling, 146
research, 23–35
rosemary, 133
rules, 116

S
safety, 116
sage, 133
salad party, 147
San Francisco Unified School
    District, 177, 181
schoolyard design, 47, 48
Scissor Salsa, 191
scope and sequence, 90
seating, 121
seed saving, 136, 151
shade, 52, 53
sheet mulching, 109
site inventory, 50
sketching, 92
slugs, 103
snails, 103
soil, 105
soil contamination, 110
soil testing, 110
solar energy, 52
spinach, 133, 135, 139, 141

squash, 133, 139
starting seeds indoors. *See*
    greenhouse
start-up funding, 40, 46
Stem Root Leaf or Fruit, 154
stewardship, 115
stormwater, 52
stove, 147
straw bales, 63
strawberries, 144
straw wattle, 63, 64
student input, 60
summer maintenance, 127
sunchokes, 140, 143
sunflowers, 133
sunlight, 53
Sun-Oven Roasted Potatoes,
    192
sun ovens, 147
supplies, 146

T
tables and benches, 121
Tamari Dijon Salad Dressing,
    186
thinning, 136
thyme, 133
tomatoes, 133, 139
tools, 129
tool shed, 70
tree rounds, 62
trees, 52
trellises, 138
turnips, 139

U
unstructured play, 34
urbanite, 65
U.S. Botanic Garden, 55

V
vandalism, 116
vermicomposting, 107, 160
victory gardens, 14
volunteer appreciation, 130
volunteers, 96, 122

W
washing station, 146
waste as a resource, 121
waste system, 146
water catchment. *See* rainwater
    harvesting
watering, 139
watershed, 167–170
weeding, 119, 120, 125
weekly garden schedule, 95
wildlife in the garden, 103, 104
wish list, 130
workdays, 129
worm composting. *See* vermi-
    composting

Y
year-round lessons, 149, 166

Z
zero waste, 145
Zip Code Seeds, 157

ABOUT THE AUTHORS

Arden Bucklin-Sporer is the executive director of the San Francisco Green Schoolyard Alliance, an advocacy organization for school gardens and outdoor classrooms. She is the director of educational gardens for the San Francisco Unified School District, and a founding partner of Bay Tree Design, Inc., a landscape architecture firm. Arden has worked with green schoolyards and public school gardens for over a decade, building an award-winning school garden program as a public school parent and working closely with school districts at the local, state, and national level. Her interest in urban agriculture is fueled by her family's organic farm and vineyard in Sonoma County, CA. Arden lives in San Francisco and Sonoma with her husband and three mostly grown sons.

Rachel Kathleen Pringle is the programs manager for the San Francisco Green Schoolyard Alliance. She is also the urban school garden liaison for Occidental Arts & Ecology Center's School Garden Teacher Training Program in Sonoma County, California. Rachel has worked in the environmental education field since moving to California in 2002. She has taught in a public school garden, integrating the curriculum into the outdoor classroom and planning events, and has also created and led workshops for garden coordinators, parents, and community members while collaborating with local environmental organizations. Before earning a Master's degree in Conservation Biology, Rachel raised cattle and kept a garden while growing up on a small farm in rural Maine.